COLLISION INVESTIGATION
FOR THE PATROL OFFICER

AF777672

Exceeds Requirements of the
California P.O.S.T.
Basic Accident Investigation Course
And
Selected Topics in P.O.S.T.'s Intermediate Traffic
Accident Investigation Course (Skid School)

BY
DAVID FAULKNER

LawTech Publishing Co., Ltd.

COLLISION INVESTIGATION
FOR THE PATROL OFFICER
By David Faulkner

Copyright ©1996-99 by ***D & K Publishing***

{All rights reserved. No part of this publication may be reproduced, stored in a retrieval system or transmitted, in any form or by any means, whether electronic, mechanical, otherwise, without prior written permission from the publisher or copyright owner.]

For seminar information or other correspondence with the author, write to:

David Faulkner
PO Box 3197
Fontana, CA 92334
e-mail: teamspyder@email.msn.com

PUBLISHED BY

LawTech Publishing Co., Ltd.
1060 Calle Cordillera, Ste. 105
San Clemente, CA 92673
Business office: (949) 498-4815
Fax: (949) 498-4858
e-mail correspondence: lawtech@fea.net
Visit our web site: www.lawtech-pub.com

See outside back cover for ordering information.

QWIK-CODE is a trademark of ***LawTech Publishing Co., Ltd.***

p. 184

Printed in the USA

ISBN: 0-915905-93-0

ACKNOWLEDGMENTS

I would like to acknowledge and thank all of the instructors who have provided me with training in the area of collision investigation and reconstruction. This would include all of the instructors from the *San Diego Police Department and Sacramento City College; Sergeant Rebecca Nations, S.D.P.D.; Officer Charles Vermillion, S.D.P.D.; Captain Val Shuppe, Ogden Utah Police Department.* There have also been a number of supervisors early in my career who recognized and encouraged my interest in the area of traffic collision investigation and enforcement. *Chief Richard Sill, Retired, Chino Police Department; Lieutenant Ed "Butch" Cisneros, Chino Police Department* (I am striving toward being the type of sergeant you both were to me, thank you!) are but just a few of those very important people.

I would also like to thank *Chief Ben Abernathy (retired), Fontana Police Department,* for my first opportunity to become a traffic officer with the city of Fontana. *Chief Ed Stout (retired), Fontana Police Department,* for the opportunities to work the various assignments during the course of my career, including my return to the traffic unit; *Chief Sam Scott, Fontana Police Department,* for allowing my continued participation in traffic related functions, including the *Street Racing Task Force* and *The Fontana Police Department Reconstruction Team;* to the entire staff of *The Fontana Police Department* for their patience and continued utilization of my skills during fatal collision responses.

A special thanks goes out to my partner on the reconstruction team, *Officer Brett Nelson, Property Clerks Nancy Beck and Marie Carter, Fontana Police Department,* for continuing to provide me with both video and photographs which were destined to be destroyed if it were not for their intervention.

I would like to acknowledge *Training Specialist Denise Garland* for her encouragement and enthusiasm toward completing this book. She was a true *godsend* when I ran into a dead end at the training center. I would like to thank everyone at the *San Bernardino County Sheriff Department's Glen Helen North Facility* for the opportunity to share this material with other officers who have a similar interest in this area of law enforcement. Several students in my past classes at the *Advanced Officer Training Facility* have provided me input during classes, which helped to shape this book for their needs.

I would especially like to thank my mother and father for their guidance and willingness to help edit the final product upon its completion. I love you both for the example you have demonstrated for me in the past and present. You are a true inspiration in my life.

DEDICATION

This book is dedicated to my wife Lori, and my children Kara & Devin (D.J.), who were extremely patient during the many long days and nights I worked on this book. Their continued prayers gave me the encouragement I needed to complete this project.

I Love you all..................

Dave December 6th, 1996

INTRODUCTION

The purpose of this book is to familiarize officers with the fundamentals of collision investigation. This book will answer those often-encountered questions while investigating and reporting collisions. The information contained in the following pages will coincide with a ***Basic Collision Investigation Course*** and will function as a quick reference guide in the coming months and years ahead. Collision investigation is not an ***"exact science"*** and therefore the material contained in this book will be left to the interpretation of the reader.

The calculations and mathematical formulas contained herein are recognized widely in the collision reconstruction community. Each of these formulas in the following pages may be found in a number of reference materials in related fields of physics and engineering. The mathematical calculations in this material have at times been ***rounded up or down*** to enhance the reader's understanding. This was decided to compensate for the vast numeric possibilities that tend to arise due to the use of different styles of calculators.

The collision scenarios pictured and discussed in these pages have been compiled from ***real life events***. Some of the details have been omitted to ease the solving of the mathematical calculations. The author's intent is to assist officers in the basics of this field of expertise. Once the investigator is armed with the necessary tools, collision investigation can become a highly interesting and educational area of police work.

THIS PAGE INTENTIONALLY LEFT BLANK

Table of Contents

Table of Contents

Chapter 10 Basic Skid Analysis (cont'd)

1

YOUR ROLE IN COLLISION INVESTIGATION

HOW DO COLLISIONS AFFECT US?

A day does not go by that we don't hear of a major collision which has occurred somewhere around us. Local radio and television news stations provide us with up to the minute reports about the flow of traffic in our area. A minor collision without injuries can disrupt the natural flow of traffic on our nation's highways. The public is very interested in what causes a collision as exemplified by the slowing of traffic in a collision area. They are also the first to complain about being diverted to an alternate roadway due to a street closure. Traffic collisions often force changes in many ways. Roadway and highway design changes have been attributed to the increased traffic flow combined with the collision rate statistics for the area examined. Daytime television commercials bombard us with ads for accident injury attorneys. The advertising attorneys in these commercials boast of the large awards they have secured for their clients. Traffic collisions cost the insurance industry, medical treatment facilities, and emergency service providers millions of dollars each year.

Yearly approximately *40,000 - 50,000* deaths are attributed to traffic collisions nationwide. Hospitals treat millions of injuries of those above reported collisions. Collisions have been found to be *the highest rate of death among males 40-50 years old.* More people have been killed in traffic collisions during the past sixty years than the total number of personnel killed during all of the wars combined in that same time period. *California has on the average 3,000 - 4,000 fatal collisions each year.* Twice as many people are killed in traffic collisions than in homicides each year. Statistically, police agencies across the nation have investigated on the average of *25 million* collisions per year.

The economic impact of collisions affects all of us. The losses in traffic collisions exceed the claims reported to insurance companies for robbery, burglary, and theft combined. Claims have been calculated to top *45 - 50 billion dollars per year* nation- wide. This impact is felt by all of us in the increase of our insurance premiums, medical, and consumer costs. Insurance fraud has also been on the rise with more staged collisions being reported. Many county district attorneys' offices have established special investigative units to combat this rise in fraudulent claims.

THE REASON FOR INVESTIGATING COLLISIONS

A large section of the general public truly believes the sole function of a traffic investigation is to assist the insurance company in repairing their respective vehicle. Many people will say to you *"My insurance company said I need a report."* State law requires police and sheriff's agencies to investigate injury and death related collisions. However, there is no law mandating agencies to investigate non-injury collisions. Many agencies have adopted policies detailing which type of collisions their officers will investigate. For example, some departments do not investigate non-injury collisions. But they do have *P.D.O.* or *Property Damage Only* report forms for those collisions which involve an unlicensed driver and require an impound. Verify your departmental guidelines which will dictate which type of collisions you will be investigating.

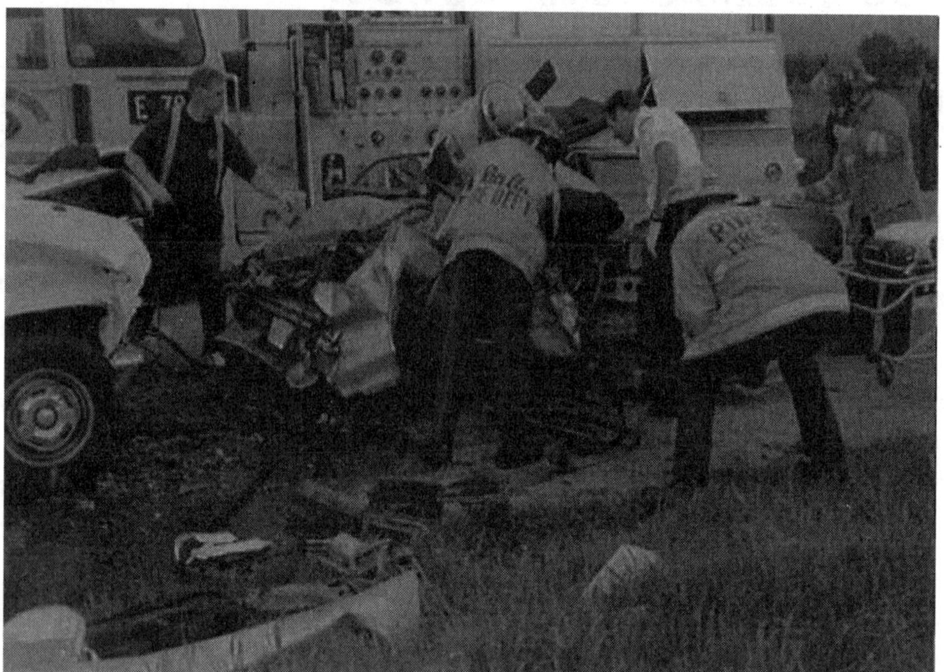

Roadway design can be a source for potential civil liability for the city or county in which you work.

One of the major reasons we investigate traffic collisions is the ever present word *"litigation."* The decisions you make at a traffic collision scene may have a far reaching impact on both the city and county in which you work. The investigators two-fold responsibility is to *look for any potential liability* to your jurisdiction and to *prevent a similar situation from reoccurring after the collision has been investigated*. You should leave no important question unanswered in the collision report. A secondary reason for your involvement in the collision process is to *properly document the collision*.

A number of agencies gain valuable information from your completed investigations. The state of California maintains records of statistical information found in your reports. This information is disseminated each year to all local and county jurisdictions. Once received, agencies apply for grant funding and can tailor their respective law enforcement action based on this information. A city engineering department may be able to justify a much needed change in the design in the roadway based on the causes of these reported collisions. Grants from the Office of Traffic Safety or OTS often require statistical information found in collision reports to justify funding of a traffic related program.

Insurance fraud has been on the rise in the past ten years. A thorough investigation may uncover those occasionally overlooked investigative clues in a fraudulently reported case. Insurance companies hope to avoid fraud by requiring a client to report a collision to their local police or highway patrol office. This may lessen the chance of a false report which can be held against the insured at a latter time in both civil and criminal court. A staged collision investigated properly will possibly highlight duplicate damage or injuries found in other reports to the same police agency.

A roadway design may be changed due to increased collisions in that location.

An often forgotten reason for collision investigation is to *promote public relations*. The public has for years expected police and sheriffs' agencies to investigate crimes. Most citizens have a common belief we investigate all traffic collisions. With departmental non-injury traffic collision guidelines changing, reportable collisions have seen a dramatic decline. For this reason alone, the reported collision data base has been reduced. Therefore, the collisions you do investigate have a much higher impact on your city or county's liability.

Be patient when contacting the public during a collision investigation. Those citizens you contact at the collision scene may have had limited exposure with your local police or sheriff's department and therefore may not understand your lack of interest in their critical incident. Explain the reason for your departmental policy and assist them in gaining the proper information. Officers often see collision investigation as a burden and feel it should not be a provided service to the public. You may be able to complete a P.D.O. report faster than trying to convince the parties why they do not need a collision report. Ask yourself this important question: *"What would I expect from an officer responding to a collision in which I was involved?"* Most of the officers reading this book would ask for the same police report as a citizen regardless of the department's individual policy. Police officers like the public, understand the insurance process moves more smoothly if this is accomplished.

A collision can completely disorient parties who suddenly find themselves in a place other than expected.

Many letters of appreciation are generated from a positive contact in a traffic-related incident. You are more likely to deal with a segment of the public that is *pro law enforcement* during a traffic collision. The public has been educated by television and the media on the caring and compassion of emergency professionals. Most people involved in a traffic collision are completely out of their respective environment and are looking to you for a strong sympathetic control of this situation.

EDUCATION AND EXPERIENCE

Traffic collision education and experience are gained by rolling up your sleeves and getting involved. Some officers will do just about anything to avoid investigating a traffic collision. Some officers say, *"I would rather investigate a major child sexual assault case than an injury traffic collision."* This sentiment permeates the law enforcement community as a whole. Traffic collision investigation is a growing field of expertise. This however, does not make the patrol officer any more comfortable with the investigation. Well investigated traffic collision reports have resulted in arrests and convictions for both vehicular manslaughter and insurance fraud.

Don't rush in your *"call to judgment"* in a collision investigation. A sloppy report may come back to haunt you in either the litigation or criminal process years after the report has been completed and filed. Take your time and ask questions if the cause of the collision appears to be complicated. Officers with traffic collision experience and knowledge are a great resource in a police or sheriff's department. Your enthusiasm and wealth of knowledge will often be sought by other officers in the field. Officers who are placed into traffic positions sometimes suddenly and without training become the departmental experts in the field of traffic enforcement and investigation. The more you investigate, the more you will learn.

Locating one item at a collision scene can make the difference and help to tell the story of how the collision occurred.

It is recommended that officers continue their education in the field of collision investigation. Begin with a Basic Collision Investigation course at your local Police or Sheriff's Academy.

A Basic Collision Investigation course will make you feel more comfortable with the topics we are about to discuss. The California Vehicle Code requires the completion of a

P.O.S.T. Basic Collision Investigation course in order to complete a *"Written Notice to Appear."*

The further you advance in the field of collision investigation, the more information will become available in your final evaluation of the collision. *Intermediate Collision Investigation* (commonly referred to as *Skid School*) follows *"Basic"* as the next course of study. *Skid School* focuses on the dynamics of how deceleration and acceleration play a role in the speed of each vehicle both prior to and after the collision. *Advanced Collision Investigation* school prepares the student for the challenges faced in collision scene analysis. *Traffic Collision Reconstruction* or *T.A.R.* combines all of this material together in a detailed analysis of the mathematical and physical aspects of the collision.

2

TRAFFIC COLLISION REPORTING

S.W.I.T.R.S.

The Highway Safety Act of 1966 caused the *State Wide Integrated Traffic Records System*, or *S.W.I.T.R.S.*, to be created. The system was in place and operational with reporting guidelines in *1972. S.W.I.T.R.S.* encourages California law enforcement agencies to send all collision reports to them, however, local agency policy will dictate their degree of participation.

C.H.P. COLLISION INVESTIGATION MANUAL

Traffic collision report writing can often times be the most confusing portion of the investigation. Determining the cause of the collision, completing the appropriate C.H.P. forms and checking the corresponding boxes can be very difficult. For this reason, the C.H.P. has published a manual that addresses each step, box and form of the traffic collision investigation report. The newest manual is available for a nominal charge and can be shipped to any law enforcement agency in the state. Many of agencies have copies of the older manuals that are still in use and are available for your use.

The Collision Investigation Manual, or *C.I.M.,* was written to establish policy and a uniform procedure for documenting traffic collisions consistent with the *California Vehicle Code*, or *CVC. 20008 CVC* requires and sets forth guidelines for the reporting of vehicular collisions within the state of California. Documentation and reporting of collisions is maintained by the *C.H.P.* for later retrieval. Each agency is encouraged to follow the suggested guidelines set forth in the manual that intended to create uniformity within the state. One can measure existing traffic patterns, law enforcement action, and roadway design with this type of information. The *C.I.M.* is a reference and instruction guide for every portion of the traffic collision report. The manual will not instruct or guide the officer in handling the collision but instead will explain each of the forms and how they should be completed.

The *C.I.M.* is divided into ten major chapters, the first of which is called *"Responsibilities and Policies." Chapter 1* defines *The California Highway Patrol's* responsibilities in collision investigation. *Chapter 1* also suggests policies for those departments that have not yet adopted one of their own. *Chapter 2* covers *"Definitions"* found in the manual and discusses their relationship to The California Vehicle Code. *Chapter 3* through *Chapter 7* provides detailed instructions for completing the *CHP 555* form and all of the additional accompanying pages. *Chapter 8* explains the use of the *CHP 555D* that will be used in a truck or bus collision that involves injury or possibly hazardous materials. *Chapter 9* includes instructions for completing the *CHP 555-03 "Property Damage Only Report"* forms. *Chapter 10* addresses the *"Form Requirements and Procedures"* as will need to be followed by your department's records unit. I will talk about these topics more thoroughly in the following pages.

RESPONSIBILITY & POLICIES

Chapter 1 dictates the policy followed by *The California Highway Patrol.* This policy is suggested but is not mandated. Most agencies in California have adopted some or all of the recommendations in this manual. The manual is written from the view of *The California Highway Patrol.* For this reason, *S.W.I.T.R.S.* recommends agencies investigate *ALL* collisions occurring on streets within your city. This would enhance the database available to the state. *S.W.I.T.R.S.* also recommends agencies investigate *ALL* non-traffic-related collisions resulting in a personal injury or death as a result of the *vehicle code.*

The first few pages in *Chapter 1* of the C.I.M. refers to the type of collision the *C.H.P.* will investigate. The following will be a comparison of the two policies which will enhance the main differences between the two entities.

C.H.P.

1. All motor vehicle collisions occurring on the freeway.
2. All motor vehicle collisions occurring on the streets and highways outside of the limits of incorporated cities.
3. All motor vehicle non-traffic collisions resulting in personal injury or death or involving a violation of *20002 CVC* in which a driver immediately fails to stop his or her vehicle at the scene and report the collision or provide notification as required by this section, or driving under the influence of alcohol or drugs occurring on a public or private property outside the limits of incorporated cities, and not within the boundaries of a military reservations, national parks, or national monuments held under the exclusive federal jurisdiction.
4. School bus collisions as defined in *12517.1 CVC,* regardless of the dollar value of the damage.
5. All motor vehicle traffic and non-traffic collisions occurring on state property patrolled as part of the safety services program or in cities contracting with the department for patrol activities.
6. All bicycle collisions occurring *on a highway* within department responsibility.

Police

1. All collisions resulting in injury or death to any person pursuant to *20008 CVC.*
2. *Property Damage Only Collisions.* All law enforcement agencies with collision reporting responsibility are encouraged to document as many collisions as possible. Local policy will determine the degree of participation.
3. Collision-related violations for prosecution.
4. Bicycle collisions.
5. Non-injury motor vehicle traffic collisions reported at the police facility. This would include counter reports as defined in *20015 CVC.*
6. Motor vehicle "*non-traffic collisions.*"

Once the two agencies' policies and responsibilities are examined, one can see the differences in the location where the report is made as well as the type of report taken. The highway patrol has the primary responsibility of investigating collisions, and the policy of their department is not flexible. Police and sheriffs' departments do have flexibility in some of the listed areas depending on the department's respective policies. The following is a line-by-line comparison of *police/sheriff vs. C.H.P.* responsibility.

	C.H.P.	***Police***
1. Injury and non-injury freeway collisions?	*Yes*	*No*
2. County roadway collisions?	*Yes*	*No*
3. State highways in the county?	*Yes*	*No*
4. State highways in the city limits?	*No*	*Yes*
5. City streets in non-contract cities?	*No*	*Yes*
6. School bus collisions with (1) pupil on board?	*Yes*	*No*
7. School bus collisions with non-pupils on board?	*No*	*Yes*
8. Non-injury traffic collisions on the street or freeway?	*Yes*	*Optional*
9. Injury traffic collisions on the street or freeway?	*Yes*	*Yes*
10. Hit and run collisions on the street or freeway?	*Yes*	*Optional*
11. Non-injury bicycle collisions on the roadway?	*Yes*	*Optional*
12. Injury bicycle collisions on the roadway?	*Yes*	*Yes*

Each agency should have a set of reporting guidelines in place based on the list from the previous pages. After this is established, the report and investigation phase begins. The first chapter of the C.I.M. refers to the type of *report* or *investigation* taken. This point is somewhat glossed over in the collision reporting process. At this point I'm sure most of you are asking, "*What's the difference?*" A majority of you is most likely writing "*investigative*" reports or a combination of these already. The following will be an example of when to use either of these formats.

Investigation

1. A motor vehicle collision results in the death of a person *on* or *off* a highway.
2. A motor vehicle traffic collision results in personal injury.
3. The collision is the result of an identifiable violation and prosecution will be sought. Moreover, the collection of evidence is required to support prosecution.
4. The collision involves a school bus. (See Chapter 2, page 2-14 C.I.M..)
5. All collisions which result in an "in-custody" arrest for a violation of 2800.1, 2800.2, 20002, or 23152 CVC.
6. An involved party is in violation of the hit-and-run provisions of 20002 CVC *on* or *off* the highway and sufficient information is available to identify the hit-and-run driver through follow-up.
   (a) A witness to the collision obtains the license plate number of the hit-and-run vehicle.
   (b) Witnesses can provide a description of the hit-and-run vehicle and reasonable physical evidence (vehicle parts, personal property, etc.) is available for a possible identification.
7. A state-owned vehicle is involved in the collision. Operational damage to the CHP vehicles will be documented according to departmental policy.

Report

1. A motor vehicle non-traffic (off highway) collision involves an injury.
2. A collision involves damage to private property and the driver is unable to notify the property owner in compliance with 20002 CVC, but notifies your department without delay. (Check you local departmental policy for guidelines in this area.)
3. A collision involves property damage only or the officer witnesses the collision-related violation and a citation is issued at the scene. (Property Damage Collisions only).
4. The collision involves a late-reported injury. (Chapter 2, page 2-8 CIM)
5. A report format would exclude a fatal or school bus collision that must be documented as an INVESTIGATION.

The information on the previous page will assist you in determining if and when a report should be taken. Report writing style and collision information will be discussed more thoroughly in the following pages.

M.A.I.T.

The California Highway Patrol has assembled a special unit to investigate major collisions involving fatalities. This team is often referred to as M.A.I.T. The name M.A.I.T. is an acronym for *Major Collision Investigation Team*. Most recently however, the teams responsibility has somewhat been expanded. The acronym itself has not changed, but the name has been modified to reflect this change. The team is now known as the *Multi-Disciplinary Collision Investigation Team*. The responsibilities and criteria by which the M.A.I.T. units may be contacted are outlined in the C.I.M. at the end of Chapter 1. The following is a synopsis of the most recent criteria required for a C.H.P call-out and can be found in Annex "M" of the C.I.M.

M.A.I.T

1. When the injury or fatal involves a "On-duty C.H.P. or Caltrans employee."
2. When the fatal or severe injury incident involves a C.H.P. aircraft.
3. When the fatal or severe injury collision occurs in which the investigation officer suspects a failure of the safety restraint system used by the injured party e.g. seatbelts, airbags and child restraint systems.
4. The following will be a partial example of collisions where a M.A.I.T. response is possible:
   (a) The collision involves four or more fatalities.
   (b) A collision with two or more fatalities involving any vehicle or combination of vehicles described in CVC 34500.
   (c) A collision involving a significant amount of hazardous materials that seriously threatens life or property.
   (d) A collision that involves a law enforcement agency where a serious or fatal injury has occurred.
   (e) A collision where the NTSB (National Traffic Safety Board) is responding.
   (f) A fatal or severe injury collision where a defect in the roadway was found to be the cause or had a major contributing factor.
   (g) The collision involves a vehicle whereas a vehicle is involved that is found to have a manufacturing defect.
   (h) A need for an in-depth speed analysis is required.

Generally the highway patrol M.A.I.T. unit will respond on a local request when there are "*four or more*" fatalities. Exceptions to this rule have been known to exist. The M.A.I.T. unit has expanded its criteria for responding in the most current version of the C.I.M. (2/98). Departments considering the use of the M.A.I.T. unit should contact the C.H.P. ahead of time to inquire about the current criteria for activating the team.

C.I.M. DEFINITIONS

Chapter 2 of the C.I.M. defines a majority of the references in the manual itself and the California Vehicle Code. The first part of this chapter centers on classifications of collisions. Most of the information is specific to movement preceding and following the collision. The most basic definitions to any material contained in the manual can be found in these pages. For example, the first few pages of this chapter defines *"Accident"* or *"Collision."* This is followed with a much more often and confused explanation of a *"stabilized situation."* We will touch on the more important definitions found in Chapter 2 of the C.I.M.

1. ***Accident or Collision:***
   An unintended event that produces *damage or injury*. The word *injury* includes *fatal injury*. *Accident* and *collision* are synonymous interchangeable words describing the event.

2. ***Area or Point of Impact:***
   The point or points at which damage or injury occurred in the collision. The *Point of Impact (POI)* could be a location where objects, vehicles, pedestrians, bicycles, or a surface come in contact with one another. A secondary term for *Point of Impact* is being used. *Area of Impact* or *AOI* is easier to articulate in an investigative report. The area is a general reference to where the officer *believes* the collision took place.

3. ***Bicycle:***
   As defined in 231 CVC, a bicycle is a device upon which any person may ride, propelled exclusively by human power through a belt, chain, or gears, and having one or more wheels. 21200 CVC states that bicycle riders are subject to the same rules of the road and reporting requirements of their vehicle counterparts when ridding upon a highway.

4. ***Chain Reaction Collisions:***
   Due to the ever-changing weather conditions, we occasionally are faced with a series of collisions in the same limited area. The event appears to be stabilizing, but the collisions are all the result of the same condition *e.g. heavy fog, rain storms, dust storms, etc.* The cause of the collision would most likely remain *unsafe speed for conditions*; however, a single collision report may be taken in this type of situation.

   Example:

   A single vehicle crosses a two-lane highway into the path of another vehicle traveling in the opposite direction. A heavy fog exists in the area and makes visibility very difficult. This, combined with vehicle speeds, leads to several other vehicles colliding with the original two vehicles involved in the collision causing a major collision. This would be documented as a single event and qualifies as a *chain reaction collision.*

Several collisions in one area as shown above may all be related to one event.

5. ***Classification or Injuries***
California classifies injuries in the following *four* categories when reporting and investigating traffic collisions:

 1. Fatal Injury.
 2. Severe Injury.
 3. Other Visible Injuries.
 4. Complaint of Pain.

6. ***Collisions After Stabilized Situations:***
A *stabilized situation* marks the *end of one event*. Nothing further will occur in so far as the event itself is concerned, but other events may follow because of subsequent actions arising from the first event. The stabilized situation may be *brief*, but *it definitely separates the end of one event from the beginning of another.*

Example:
A truck carrying a load of pipe collides with a vehicle. The collision itself has stopped, but the rescue personnel are on scene attempting to remove the occupants from both vehicles. During the rescue operation, the load shifts and falls into the path of a passing vehicle. The original collision event involving the truck has *stabilized*, and the shifting load which resulted in a second collision is considered a new and separate event.

7. ***Counter Report or Citizen Report:***
These terms can be considered as synonymous in the *C.I.M.* Each refers to a "Property Damage Only" collision reported by the involved parties at the police facility or C.H.P. office. Many agencies have posted directions for completing the *P.D.O.* forms in the front desk area and ask the involved parties to compete the forms themselves. Counter Reports are *not* processed into the *Statewide Integrated Traffic Records System* (SWITRS) database files.

8. ***Courtesy report:***
A report taken by a police agency outside of the area where the collision first took place. Agencies may be willing to assist the responsible agency upon request through the watch commander.

9. ***Deliberate Intent***
An *intentional act* that directly or indirectly involves a motor vehicle in transport that purposely causes damage to property or injury to any person. If the intended act results in other injury or damage that appears to go beyond the original intent, the additional event is considered to be *accidental* and therefore is considered a motor vehicle *traffic collision.* Malicious mischief, such as throwing objects from an overpass is considered deliberate intent even though the act was not directed toward a specific person. The following examples are not considered traffic collisions.

    Suicide or Self Inflicted Injury:
    You locate a female behind the wheel of a vehicle stopped on the railroad tracks after a commuter train collision. The female driver tells you her intent was to commit suicide because her spouse is ridding on the train with which she was struck. This is not considered a traffic collision by definition and therefore a traffic collision report should not be taken.

    Homicide, Injury or Damage Purposely Inflicted:
    A pedestrian was struck by a vehicle that fled the scene prior to your arrival. A witness at the scene informs you he saw the suspect vehicle stop and the driver of the vehicle revs the engine for a moment. The suspect drove his vehicle in a manner that looked as if he (the suspect) was aiming for the victim. The scenario described above would not qualify as a motor vehicle traffic collision and instead would be investigated as a 245 PC (Assault with a Deadly Weapon).

    Staged Traffic Collisions:
    Intentional acts that result in at first what appears to be a traffic collision. The overt actions that caused the incident were intentional and known to the party who staged the collision. Therefore the resulting damage and injuries are not classified as a traffic collision.

10. ***Driver:***

One who is in *physical control of the vehicle*. A driver does not include a *tillerman* or other person who in an auxiliary capacity assists the driver in the steering operation of any fire fighting apparatus. Such persons are considered *passengers*.

11. ***Highway***

A road publicly maintained and open to the use of the public for purposes of vehicular travel. The term Highway includes streets, shoulders and sidewalks. A portion of the Highway that is closed to vehicular travel such as a construction zone or an area closed during a traffic collision investigation, *no longer* meets the definition of a Highway. Any collisions occurring in the above-described areas would be considered *motor vehicle non-traffic collisions*.

12. ***In Transport***

A vehicle when it is used primarily for moving persons or property (including the vehicle itself) from one place to another. A motor vehicle is considered *In Transport* when in the roadway, whether moving, stopped, stalled, disabled or abandoned. Motor vehicles in designated parking areas, shoulders, or off of the highway are considered *In Transport* only when moving.

Note: For the purposes of this definition, a vehicle is considered to be in the roadway when a passing vehicle that is traveling entirely in the roadway could strike it.

13. ***Injury***

Fatal Injury – Death as a result of the injuries sustained in a traffic collision that occurs within 30 days of the original incident. An unborn fetus of a pregnant female involved in a collision will be counted as a fatal injury if the coroner *attributes the death to the collision* and the fetus is greater than *20 weeks* old at the time.

Fatal Injury is a death from injuries sustained in a collision and that occurs within 30 days of the original incident.

<u>Severe Injury</u> – An injury other than those categorized as a fatal injury that result in broken, dislocated or distorted limbs, severe lacerations or when unconscious when taken from the scene.

<u>Other Visible Injuries</u> – Includes bruises that appear discolored or swollen in places where the body has taken a "blow." This would include black eyes and bloody noses and abrasions (skinned knees, shines, knuckles and shins).

<u>Complaint of Pain</u> – This category could contain authentic internal or otherwise nonviable injuries and fraudulent claims of injury. Examples of these might include, but not necessarily be limited to the following:

- Persons who seem dazed, confused or incoherent.
- Persons who are limping, but do not have any visible injuries.
- Any party who is known to have been unconscious as a result of the collision, even though he/she is now recovered.
- Persons, who state they want to be listed as injured, but do not appear to be injured.

14. ***Intersection***
The area located within the prolongation of the lateral curb lines, or if none, the lateral boundary lines of the roadways of two highways that join one another at approximately *"right angles."* It is also an area where two vehicles travelling upon different highways joining at any other angle may come in conflict with one another. When the distance along a roadway between two areas meeting this criteria is less than 10 meters (33 feet), the two areas and the roadway connecting them is considered to be parts of a single intersection *365 CVC.*

15. ***Lane Numbering and Identification:***
A vast majority of the public commonly refers to the lanes of the roadway as *"the fast lane and the slow lane."* Traffic lanes are numbered from the inside or center of the roadway toward the shoulder. Most four-lane roadways would consist of *two lanes* in each direction. This can be expanded to cover a multitude of lanes counting from the inside toward the shoulder of the roadway

16. ***Late Reported Collisions***
A fatal or injury collision where the involved vehicles and all parties no longer remain at the scene and documentation is requested away from the scene where the incident occurred. The investigating officer shall determine if the collision was reported after the first available opportunity to make such a report before indicating the status as a *"Late Report.."* Late reported collisions may be reported anytime up to *"one year"* from the date of occurrence. Slight movement away from the scene to clear the roadway or driving to a safer location is *not* considered a *Late Reported Collision.*

17. ***Legal Intervention:***

This definition has seen a decline over the years as law enforcement agencies tighten their respective policies in this area due to liability. Situations do occur where *legal intervention* may be the only option at the officer's disposal. The traffic investigator should be prepared to provide his/her reasoning for determining the incident in this manner. Injury and damage caused by *legal intervention* while agencies attempt to *apprehend* a suspect may result in what appears at first to be a collision. Once the intervention has been applied and the act has gone beyond the intended outcome, the excessive acts can be considered *accidental* and qualify as a motor vehicle collision.

Includes:

- *Roadblocks set up to stop the fleeing offender.* The suspect vehicle collides with the police units either intentionally or unintentionally as a result of avoiding the roadblock.
- A police unit conducts a *blocking maneuver* and attempts to *force* the violator's vehicle to stop. The vehicles collide as a direct result of this act.
- A police unit intentionally collides with a pursued vehicle in an attempt to terminate the pursuit.
- The suspect vehicle loses control and collides as a direct result of the *officer using a firearm against the occupants.*

Excludes:

- An uninvolved party to the roadblock *loses control* and crashes into the roadblock.
- The driver of the *fleeing suspect vehicle loses* control due to his own speed and collides with an uninvolved vehicle in the pursuit.
- The pursuing *police unit loses control* and collides with another vehicle, a pedestrian or a fixed object.
- The pursuing officer *unintentionally collides* with the vehicle he or she is pursuing at the time.

18. ***Motor Vehicle***

A mechanically or electrically powered device *not operated on rails*, upon which or by which any person or property may be transported or drawn upon a highway. A motor vehicle does not include a self propelled wheel chair, invalid tricycle, or motorized quadricycle when operated by a person, by reason of their physical disability is otherwise unable to move about as a pedestrian.

Examples:

- Passenger cars, trucks, van, or sport utility vehicles.
- Commercial truck carriers.
- Farm equipment e.g. tractors and combines.
- A Moped is considered a vehicle for collision reporting purposes.

- Equipment such as trailers coaster sleds or wagons whether towed or pushed by a motor vehicle is considered part of the vehicle even if the equipment is detached while in motion.

19. ***Motor Vehicle Non-traffic Collision:***
A collision involving a vehicle in-transport occurring entirely in a place *off the highway.*

Examples:

- A collision occurring off the highway on private property.
- Off highway collisions not involving a motor vehicle in transport such as a plane or train related crash not meeting the definition of a *vehicle in transport* become the responsibility of the local police or sheriff's agency.
- Any organized race event such as a professional *NHRA*® top fuel competition involving a death or personal injury.
- An injury or death resulting from an activity while on a *designated parade route.*
- Property damage, injury or death, which occurs during an *agricultural operation.*
- A death or personal injury occurring on the grounds of an industrial plant *while operating a forklift.*
- An injury or death which occurs during an officially sponsored bicycle racing event. The race event must take place on a *closed course.*

20. ***Motor Vehicle Traffic Collision:***
Any motor vehicle collision occurring on a highway, or which begins on a highway and terminates on an adjacent roadway. This would include a vehicle movement which begins on a roadway and continues off the roadway where the impact occurs.

Examples:

- A motor vehicle *in-transport* spills a load on the roadway, which either strikes or is struck by a passing vehicle. The vehicle carrying the load *does not* need to be involved in the actual collision.
- A motor vehicle *in-transport* is involved in a *non-collision* event. This could include a number of varying circumstances, which would not fit the normal guidelines of a motor vehicle collision.
- A person being thrown against a portion of the vehicle and sustaining injuries.
- Injuries sustained in a vehicle collision resulting from a fire.
- Passengers which fall from the vehicle prior to a collision.
- Damage to a jack-knifed commercial truck.
- Damage to a tow truck or trailer being towed by a motor vehicle.
- A school bus transporting students strikes a bump in the roadway, causing a student to strike his/her face on a seat.

21. ***Non Contact Involved Parties:***

A vehicle, driver, bicycle or pedestrian that does not make actual contact with the damaged vehicle in the collision. The party who fits this criteria should be considered an involved party under the following circumstances:

- The driver, bicycle rider or pedestrian commits a traffic violation, which directly contributes to the cause of the collision.
- The traffic violation can be corroborated by an independent witness, physical evidence, or statements of the *non-contact* party themselves.
- This *excludes* a party *attempting to evade a lawful arrest* unless the listed criteria are met. The mere fact the party is being pursued is not sufficient to make that person a party in the collision. The actions should be included in your report.

Example:

A pedestrian crosses the street directly into the path of a passing motor vehicle and causes the driver of the vehicle to swerve to avoid a collision. The vehicle then strikes a secondary vehicle or fixed object. The pedestrian clearly violated *21954(a) CVC* which states in part: *"...Every pedestrian upon the roadway at any point within a marked crosswalk or within an unmarked crosswalk at an intersection shall yield the right-of-way to all vehicles close enough to constitute an immediate hazard..."*

22. ***On-duty Emergency Vehicle Collision:***

This selection in the body of the traffic collision report would be checked when a peace officer meets all of the criteria as defined in *Penal Code Section 830.1, 830.2, 830.3, 830.4, 830.5, 830.6,* and *all* related subsections. The collision is noted on the officer's driving record; however, the notation *"on-duty emergency vehicle"* is printed just below the location where the collision occurred. The sole purpose of this notation is to alert the insurance industry, the officer, sheriff's deputy, CHP officer, or fireman should be provided the protection under the *Insurance Code Sections 488.5, 557.5, and 669.5*. The vehicle must meet all of the requirements of a *"on-duty emergency vehicle"* as defined in *165 CVC*. The emergency vehicle may be marked or unmarked and will be operated by those officers, firefighters, or paramedics in the *performance of their duties.*

Officers operating emergency vehicles are protected from having the collision count against their DMV records.

23. ***Passenger:***

A passenger is any person *inside* or *upon* a vehicle, excluding the driver. This includes a person *behind the wheel of a parked motor vehicle.*

24. ***Pedestrian:***

Any person who is *"afoot"* or who is using a means of conveyance propelled by human power other than a bicycle. Pedestrian includes any person who is operating a *self propelled wheel chair, invalid tricycle, or motorized quadricycle* and by reason of their physical disability is *unable to move about as a pedestrian (467 CVC).*

25. ***Roadway***

That portion of a highway improved, designed or ordinarily used for vehicular travel *530 CVC.* In the event a highway includes two or more separate roadways, the term roadway refers to either of the separate roadways, but all such roadways collectively.

26. ***School Bus Collisions:***

The school bus must be involved in a property or personal injury traffic collision and involve the following:

- The school bus must meet the definition of a school bus as defined in *545 CVC* while transporting at least *one pupil at or below the 12th grade.* The bus must be enroute *to or from a school function.*
- A *school pupil activity bus* as defined in *546 CVC.*
- A *Youth bus,* as defined in *680 CVC,* while transporting at least *one pupil* or student *at or bellow the 12th grade level.* The bus must also be enroute *to or from a non-school related youth activity* within *25 miles* of the school.
- A *General Public Paratransit vehicle* as defined in *336 CVC* while transporting *any pupil* or student *at or below the 12th.*

Any collision which appears to satisfy these parameters becomes the responsibility of the California Highway Patrol and shall be investigated as directed by the **C.I.M.**. A *Non-school bus collision* is a collision without any pupils on board as defined on the previous page. These collisions will become the responsibility of the local police or sheriffs department.

CHP will investigate school bus collisions when one or more pupils at or below the 12th grade are on board.

27. ***Shoulder***
The portion of the road next to the roadway used for accommodation of stopped vehicles, for emergency stops and lateral support of the roadway structure itself.

28. ***Staged Traffic Collisions***
Those that are intentionally planned and contrived for fraudulent purposes.

29. ***Tow Away:***
The collision becomes a tow away collision when at least one of the involved vehicles is damaged to the extent it cannot be driven away from the scene under its own power. The easiest way to remember the difference between the two (tow-away and non-tow- away) is to *exclude* damage which is not severe enough to justify a *quick fix* at the scene. An example of this would be a vehicle in which the fender is damaged and could be pulled away from the tire allowing the vehicle to be driven away from the scene. Tow-away would also *exclude the following*:

    - The vehicle is towed due to the *incapacitation of the driver.*
    - Parts on the vehicle *not necessary* to the safe operation of the vehicle no longer work, *e.g. doors, trunk, hood, etc.*
    - A vehicle has caught on fire as a result of the impact.
    - The vehicle is towed away from the scene for a condition not resulting from the impact in the collision such as *4000(a) 1 CVC (registration) or 22651(p) CVC (unlicensed driver impounds).*
    - A vehicle was rolled in the collision, but has been up righted and can now be driven away from the scene.

30. ***Uninvolved Party:***
A party who has contributed to the collision, but sustained *no damage* or *injury* as a result of the incident. No real evidence exists to substantiate the party most at fault in the collision committed the violation which caused the collision. An independent witness does not exist to verify the party's statement by the uninvolved driver.

Examples:

- A vehicle stops for a pedestrian in a marked crosswalk. A vehicle traveling in the same direction attempts to avoid colliding with the vehicle which has stopped in front of him and swerves into a vehicle in the adjacent lane. The party who stopped initially did not violate the vehicle code by stopping for the pedestrian in the crosswalk. The driver did not contribute to the collision which followed as a result of yielding for the pedestrian. He therefore is considered an *uninvolved party.*

- A vehicle is traveling at the posted speed limit for the area. A vehicle traveling in the same direction makes a passing maneuver and does not have the clearance necessary to complete the movement safely. The passing maneuver results in a traffic collision. The party who was passed by the speeding vehicle did not contribute to the collision and would be considered an *uninvolved party.*

31. ***Witness***
A person other than a party or passenger that was not involved in the traffic collision and who can provide an unbiased account of the circumstances leading up the collision. The witness may have observed such relevant details as alcohol consumption, either before or after the collision took place.

PROPERTY DAMAGE ONLY

The property damage only report is relatively new in the collision investigation world. This form has simplified the basic investigation of a traffic collision. The C.H.P. was the first agency in the state of California to introduce this format. Most agencies have since adopted a variation of this triplicate form with a few minor changes. The Fontana Police Department has created its own form of the C.H.P. property damage only report. Fontana Police have since expanded the use of this form to include *hit and run* collisions with no suspect information. The following will be a example of the possible uses of this form as dictated by the S.W.I.T.R.S manual.

P.D.O. requirements

- ***One*** or ***two party*** collisions.
- ***No injury*** or ***fatal*** collisions.
- ***No Prosecution*** is anticipated.

CHECK THE BOX

The second page of the C.H.P. 555 form is a *check the box format* which helps the reviewing officer to determine the cause of the collision *at a glance*. These *check the box* areas can greatly support your analysis of how the collision occurred. Take your time in choosing the factors which best describe the weather, area lighting, roadway conditions, and traffic control devices. Any of these factors may be discerned by a sharp attorney as the city or county's responsibility. For instance the lighting or lack thereof may be extremely important in an auto/pedestrian collision. A lawyer may try to argue the lighting in the area was not adequate for the roadway conditions.

Be fair in your selection of these issues and be prepared to explain your reason for choosing your marked selections. Many officers have been surprised in depositions years after the collision report was completed. An attorney may ask you to explain your choices on the second page of your collision report. Your narrative should *go hand in hand* with any reference to unique conditions on this form. The asterisk in this selection area reminds the investigating officer that a narrative reference is necessary.

MOVEMENT PRECEDING THE COLLISION

"*Movement preceding the collision*" is found in the *check the box* area of the C.H.P. 555 form. This specific reference is made to the movement *just before the collision.* Several suggestions can be found in this area to assist the officer in making the appropriate choice, *e.g. stopped, making a left turn, changing lanes, backing, slowing, etc.* The officer must choose the movement which best describes what had occurred. When two complete and separate movements apply, select the movement which more likely caused the collision. A turning movement may be more appropriate if the passing maneuver was safe.

Two investigating officers may come to different conclusions when choosing the appropriate selections in the *check the box* area of the report, but try to be as accurate as possible. Locate the *C.H.P. 555 (face sheet)* and *injury/witness* sheets and examine each of the boxes to familiarize yourself with the possible selections available to you. Each of the areas on the form has a corresponding reference in the C.I.M. For those officers using *C.S.T.A.R.S. (Computerized State Traffic Accident Reporting System)*, the entire C.I.M. manual is loaded with the software via the *help mode.*

INJURY & WITNESS PAGE

The C.H.P. Injury/Witness page is used to document injuries of those involved in the collision. A box also exists to document *fatal* collisions on this form. Witness information can be added to this form in the same manner. The form is somewhat self-explanatory and requests the *name, address, date of birth, and the telephone number* of all listed parties. A space can be found just below each name for an explanation of the parties' injuries and where the injured parties were transported. The C.H.P. Injury/Witness form also asks where the injured parties, witnesses, and passengers were seated in the vehicle. A reference can be found about *ejection and safety equipment.* Once this information is obtained, refer to the upper rear portion of the C.H.P. 555 for the correct corresponding code which should be placed in this area. The Injury/Witness page is discussed further in Chapter 5 of the C.I.M.

REPORT WRITING

Annex "A" of the C.I.M. provides the investigating officer with several examples of report narratives. The samples in the manual are those which fit C.H.P. guidelines. These narratives may be used as a *road map* for completing your report. Each agency and officer will develop his or her own report writing style and format.

Earlier in this chapter different report formats were discussed. Each of these types of reports, whether *investigative* or *summary*, has a specific set of headings. The headings you utilize in these reports may vary depending on your departmental policies. The following will be a sample of the headings, which are being used by a variety of departments across California and have been recommended by S.W.I.T.R.S.

Investigative Format:

Facts

Notification:

- The time, type of call, and the location from which you responded.
- A statement that all of the speeds and measurements are approximate, and the manner in which these were obtained, *e.g. roll-a-tape, pacing, steel tape, etc.*

Scene Description:

- Roadway description including the surface type, elevation, and lane configuration.
- Any relative fixed objects.
- A description and type of traffic control devices.

Party Information:

- The party's name, how he/she was identified, and how it was determined he/she was the driver.
- The location of the vehicle they were driving.
- Any observed mechanical defects you notice on the vehicle, which in your opinion may have contributed to the collision.

Physical Evidence:

- Type, location, and length of any skidmarks located at the scene.
- Debris and any vehicle parts relative to the impact.
- Any other physical evidence unless listed in the factual diagram.
- Disposition of the evidence collected at the scene.

Hit and Run:

- Describe the suspect vehicle, driver, clothing worn and possible direction of travel from the scene.
- Can the witness or involved driver identify the suspect or suspect's vehicle if seen again. If they can identify the suspect, can they place him or her behind the wheel of the suspect vehicle?
- Summary of follow-up actions or explanations as to why follow-up was not possible.

Hazardous Materials:

- Trade and chemical names if located.
- Presence or absence of posted placards, labels, and shipping papers.

- The type of packaging used.
- The cleanup contractor, method, and disposition of the material once contained.

Other Information:

- Drivers license restrictions, physical defects, etc. of the parties involved.

Statements:

- Identify all parties and witnesses by number and last name.
- Include both the *questions and answers* if this type of interview is performed.
- When the party or witness writes a statement, indicate *"statement attached."*
- Statements do not need to be repeated if they are similar to a statement received from another party.
- Indicate "*no statement*" was obtained if this applies due to the parties' injuries, death, or flight from the scene.
- Indicate the witnesses' location when observations were made.

Opinions and Conclusions

Summary:

- Provide your opinion as to how the collision occurred based on the physical evidence, statements, and other factors.
- The description of how the collision occurred should be complete.

Area of Impact (A.O.I.)

- State how the A.O.I. was determined using physical evidence, statements, and debris.
- Locate the A.O.I. with a minimum of *two measurements*.
- Repeat this process for each additional A.O.I.

Intoxication:

- The parties action(s) in the collision.
- Any field sobriety tests given or make a reference to an attached additional page if applicable.
- Explain how the erratic driving and state of intoxication where proven, *e.g.* physical evidence, statements by witnesses, or an admission by the driver.
- Location, description, and identification of the person who discovered the alcohol found either in the vehicle or at the scene.

Cause:

- A decision and explanation of who was at fault and how that fault was determined by the primary collision factor.
- In *felony* cases, include how the act of neglect was the proximate cause of the injury.

Recommendations:

- List any follow-up action needed.
- Include how the *act* was determined to be *the proximate cause of the injury or death* in a *felony case.*
- Should the case be forwarded to the District Attorneys office?
- If you have don't have any recommendations, write *none.*

REPORT FORMAT

Notification:

- List the time you received the call, the type of call, the location from which you responded, and the time you arrived on the scene.
- A reference should be made in the report that *all speeds and measurements are approximate.*
- Explain how the measurements were taken, e.g. using a steel tape, roll-a-tape, or pacing.

Statements:

- Add statements if needed.

Summary:

- Give your opinion in a sequential order of what took place and how the collision occurred.

  Examples:
  - Vehicle direction, highway description, lane of travel, and speeds.
  - Actions of the drivers.
  - Defective vehicle equipment.
  - If applicable, identify which of the drivers was H.B.D. but *not under the influence*. List which tests, if any, assisted you in making this determination.

A.O.I.

- List the location of the A.O.I. and what evidence was present to support it.

Cause:

- The officer should explain *why* the collision occurred by *identifying the driver action, corresponding vehicle code violation (CVC), and how this decision was made.*

SUPPLEMENTAL FORMAT

The C.H.P. 556 was created to serve as a report narrative form. This form can also be used to complete supplemental reports to the original collision investigation. You are not limited to this form, but instead may use your department's report narrative pages. Departments who utilize computer generated report narratives may print the supplemental report narrative on plain white paper. Unlike many crime reports, a page does not exist for additional witnesses' names and reporting party information. You may add the *"injury/witness page"* or simply place the party's name in the body of the narrative. I indent at the end of the party's statement and include his/her name, address, DOB, and phone number rather than add an *"injury/witness page"*. The following will be a partial list of possible uses for a supplemental report.

- A change in the severity of the collision from an *injury to a fatal.*
- A change in the designation of the collision from a *"fatal to other cause"* due to additional investigative factors learned after the initial report has been filed, e.g. heart attack, stroke, etc.
- The status of the collision changes from *property damage only* to a confirmed *injury collision.*
- One of the driver's status changes as a result of information learned from the *autopsy,* e.g. sobriety.
- The identification of the driver was not previously known due to a *hit and run* collision.
- A change is necessary from a *"motor vehicle collision"* to a *"motor vehicle non-traffic collision."*

TRUCK/BUS COLLISION SUPPLEMENTAL REPORT

Chapter 8 of the C.I.M. has been added to clarify and define the use of C.H.P. 555D form when the collision involves trucks, busses or hazardous materials. Effective October 1st, 1998, all agencies *must* prepare a C.H.P. 555D for all qualifying collisions involving commercial motor vehicles. The form once completed will need to be attached to the rear of your investigative reports. The form is explained in it's entirety including references on how to fill out each one of the boxes on the form itself.

The officer at the scene must decide if the vehicles involved in the collision qualify as a reportable incident under the guidelines of the National Governors' Association (NGA) and if a C.H.P. 555D is required. The responding officer also must determine if the vehicles involved meet the definition of a truck, bus and if so, whether the damage and injuries are severe enough to fit the listed criteria. The definitions of the above mentioned vehicles are contained on the back of the C.H.P. 555D to assist the investigating officer. There are *two* conditions that the officer must consider when determining if the incident must be reported as outlined above. *BOTH* of these conditions must be met.

1. **Qualifying Vehicles –** The collisions must involve either
   (a) *A truck having at least six tires in contact with the roadway surface;* or
   (b) *A vehicle displaying a hazardous materials placard;* or
   (c) *A bus with seating for more than 15 persons including the driver.*
   and…

2. **Severity of the Collision** – The collision must result in
   (a) *At least one fatality; or*
   (b) *At least one injury severe enough for the injured person to require transportation from scene for immediate medical attention; or*
   (c) *At least one involved vehicle sustaining disabling damage (damage other than flat tire which is sufficient to prevent the vehicle from being driven away without repair) or a disabling event (an event requiring the vehicle to be moved, uprighted, or otherwise assisted by emergency equipment).*

NOTE: *The severity criterion applies to any vehicle or person involved in the collision. If collision is determined to be reportable, a separate C.H.P. 555D must completed for each qualifying vehicle.*

FORM REQUIREMENTS & PROCEDURES

Chapter 10 of the C.I.M. outlines how the appropriate report forms should be handled once completed. This chapter also explains the distribution and the retention of those reports by your agency and records division. Each department's records division must follow the guidelines printed in this manual for returning the completed reports to the Sacramento office of the C.H.P.

3

COLLISION SCENE MANAGEMENT

YOUR RESPONSIBILITY AT A COLLISION SCENE

Each day officers are dispatched to the scene of collisions in our various cities and counties. But not often do they think about their *awesome responsibility*. The public, media, and fellow officers count on our experience and leadership in bringing these large-scale scenes under control. The response usually begins with a radio broadcast or *"Tom four: respond to a reported major injury traffic collision on Poplar Ave. south of Slover Ave."* This response can become *"routine"* for some officers, but this was the author's first assignment after becoming a member of the Fontana Police Department Traffic Unit in 1986. Starting his first evening excited and ready to tackle the traffic problems of his city. What he found shortly after *2000 hours* on that early February night was a *fatal traffic collision.*

Upon arrival, he located a Chevy El Camino along the west curb line of the street which had collided with the rear of a flatbed semi-tractor trailer combination. The trailer of this truck was carrying three large heavy sewer pipes. The impact was so great that it moved the parked semi tractor and trailer *five feet forward*. He was completely overwhelmed to say the least. He exited his police unit and found the driver crawling away from the vehicle with multiple fractures protruding from the lower portion of his leg. The female passenger *exhaled her last breath* as he arrived to check on her in the vehicle. She was unrestrained and had broken her neck upon impacting the windshield.

Fortunately, he had help from other officers at the scene. He had received virtually *no formal training in the area of collision investigation*. The officers present looked to him and hoped he could piece together what had happened. The department issued him a pair of *"traffic wings"*, and suddenly he was granted knowledge in collision investigation. He attended a *Basic Collision Investigation* class shortly after the collision and realized things could have been done differently. He looks back on this collision every time he speaks at a *Basic Traffic Collision* course. All of us have been in this situation at one time or another, facing a major event which tests our abilities to solve the problem at hand. No real hard and fast rules apply to handling a traffic collision scene. We each have a list of priorities which comes into play at the scene. This chapter will be dedicated to helping you set those priorities in motion with the basic fundamentals of good *traffic scene management.*

PROTECTION OF THE SCENE

Once you receive the call on your *mobile data terminal (M.D.T.)* or *radio*, begin to reflect on the scene as you might find it. Note the time the call is received and the location from which you are responding. Other units will most likely be responding to assist you if the collision is found to involve an *injury*. If this is not the case, be prepared to ask for additional help if needed. The list below will be a suggested set of guidelines for you to follow upon arriving at the scene.

Priorities at the scene:

- After arriving at the scene, position your police unit in such a manner as to *protect the parties and the scene in general.*
- Check with *all* involved parties and verify if anyone is injured or is in need of medical attention.
- Direct additional responding units to locations *which will assist you in controlling the scene*. This will include safely directing traffic around the perimeter of the collision.
- Attempt to locate any potential witnesses as soon as possible. This can be delegated to a secondary officer if you are busy managing the scene. Early contacts can sometimes persuade the witnesses to stay at the scene until it becomes more manageable.
- Place your flare pattern in such a way that it will protect you and the rescue personnel. Fire and paramedic personnel have a tendency to park at the scene without much concern for traffic flow. Once the situation begins to stabilize, don't be afraid to contact the drivers and ask them politely to reposition their respective vehicles.
- How serious are the injuries in the collision? Other assistance might be required such as your departmental *reconstruction team.*
- How many tow trucks are needed and will they be *impounds* or *owners requests?* If the vehicles will be impounded under *22655.5 CVC* or any of the other *22651 CVC* sections, you may consider detailing this work to another officer at the scene. Towing and vehicle storage can remove the investigating officer away from his responsibilities at the scene.
- Will the *air rescue unit* be responding? Have you picked out a suitable location for the *landing zone?* If you are requested to assist the fire department personnel in this selection, have you considered *traffic flow, pedestrian safety, and potential danger to officers at the scene?* Once the selection is made, assess the need for additional units to help close the area.

Landing Zones need to be selected with the safety of the surrounding officers and public in mind.

DEVICES FOR TRAFFIC CONTROL

Many years ago officers had a very difficult task in directing and controlling traffic at a collision scene. The amount of traffic on the roadway combined with the curiosity factor of the public can distract drivers from operating their vehicle in a safe manner. The 1990's however have seen a major change in the available equipment utilized in traffic scene management. For example, the *"arrow stick"* is being added to the majority of the newer style police light bars. These traffic directional light controls can more effectively gain the attention of the curious motorist. Once the attention is gained, the device directs the motorist toward the area intended for their travel. This will also keep the passing motorists from asking questions as they pass the collision scene. These light bars and *"arrow sticks"* are only effective if the officer utilizes them properly. If you have not used one of these devices, it is recommend that you become familiar with how they work before responding to a scene. Again, think about the area where the collision occurred while responding to the location. You may be able to picture how traffic will be directed around the scene during your approach to the location.

Familiarize yourself with the traffic control equipment on your police unit.

Safety is a primary concern in traffic scene management. Officers have been injured or killed while setting flare patterns and directing traffic at these scenes. Officers wearing dark blue uniforms are very difficult to see due to the non-reflective nature of the material. Many officers have had close calls while directing traffic at a collision scene. Make use of any available lighting that will help illuminate both yourself and the roadway. Remember the public will be distracted while passing through a collision location and will not see you in the roadway. Several departments have started issuing an orange striped vest to the officers that can be worn over their uniforms for higher visibility.

Consider the placement of your vehicle in respect to where you are standing in the roadway. The distraction of the rotating light bar may also divert attention away from you. Roadway and weather conditions may add to the visibility problem motorists have in seeing you, both during the day and evening. Consider your placement in the proximity to the damaged vehicles. Do the vehicles detract from my ability to be seen? The passing motorist will see you secondary to the interest they have in viewing the damaged vehicles. Most officers no longer carry whistles, but this may very much get the attention of the daydreaming motorist. A whistle may also be viewed as less aggressive than yelling at a motorist.

Position yourself carefully among the vehicles and debris. Officers can be very difficult to see at a collision scene.

The following will be an excerpt from a *death notification* found on the *Internet* which detailed how an officer was killed while directing traffic at a collision scene in New York.

> ***"An officer assigned to the NYPD's Highway Unit 2 in Brooklyn was killed by a passing vehicle........The collision occurred shortly after the P.M. shift as the officer was putting down flares in the roadway....The officer was talking with another motorist when he was struck by a passing Chevy Blazer.........The officer's body was essentially cut in half by the impact..."***

We have all experienced the frustration of those drivers who *cannot quite understand what we think is a simple flare pattern.* What might be simple in appearance to us as law enforcement officers may not be interpreted as simple to the *hypnotic state of the average commuter.* A flare pattern or police unit itself will not handle the traffic flow without some help from you. Many officers set a flare pattern and become distracted by the collision scene as well. They suddenly find the flare pattern has burned out, and vehicles are beginning to drive around the police unit. The officer becomes frustrated and finds himself yelling at the motorist such things as *"Why do think this patrol car is parked here with all of these pretty red and blue lights on?"* Realistically, what is the citizen supposed to do in this situation? They realize by your tone and appearance that they have been considered the *most stupid human on earth.*

Patience appears to be the best way to direct traffic. If you assume the motorist has no clue, then you will not become nearly as angry when they exhibit this behavior. Also be prepared for the passing motorist to ask questions. Many of these citizens have been driving this same roadway for many years and suddenly you are changing their driving pattern. They simply may be looking for an alternative route. A question from a motorist may cause a slight back-up, but they will soon become frustrated as well due to the unfamiliarity of the area. This will lead them to locate another officer who may not be ready for their insistent attitude.

You are the best form of traffic control. Try to be patient and understanding when dealing with the confused public.

A supervisor may make the traffic flow outside the collision scene *more important* than the incident itself. Respectfully advise the supervisor the roadway needs to remain closed to protect the collision scene. Plan your flare pattern, unit placement, or barricades in such a way as to facilitate the smoothest flow of traffic possible for the problem at hand. Additionally try not to become frustrated at the motorist who appears to be *totally lost.* Traffic direction can be one of the most challenging aspects of our job as law enforcement officers. A secondary problem in traffic flow outside of the scene is *"rubber neckers"* There have been many secondary collisions outside of the original collision scene due to the lack of attention by the passing drivers. Your traffic direction and constant urging of the traffic flow can sometime avert this type of activity. You may need to remind the passing drivers to *"pay attention"* as they slow to view the incident.

FACTORS WHICH MAY AFFECT YOUR DECISION

Several factors may influence your decision in traffic control placement and equipment. Such things as highway design, roadway speeds, environmental factors affecting visibility *(fog, smog, fire, and smoke)*, and hazardous material may all come into play when making a decision of how to contain the scene. Each one of these factors must be equally weighed in the planning process. Anyone of the above mentioned factors could severely impact your perimeter of the scene to be contained. This evaluation must be made in your first few minutes of arrival if at all possible. Interested parties, the press, and additional emergency rescue personnel can quickly overrun the scene.

Damaged power poles can potentially electrocute the responding officers or people passing through the scene.

Check for downed power lines that may become a major electrical hazard to the drivers, bystanders, and responding rescue personnel. Passing drivers have been known to collide with telephone and power lines which were not properly protected after the first officers arrived on the scene. Don't rely on the passing motorist to perceive the hazard at hand. For instance, in a very heavy rainstorm, the flare pattern or police unit may become visible to approaching traffic just a short distance before they observe you.

Communication at the collision scene is vital to your survival. The size and nature of the collision can overwhelm even the most experienced and even-tempered officer. Collision scenes are filled with large equipment that make a tremendous amount of noise. Something as simple as a tow-truck can become distracting in your attempt to communicate with other officers. These sounds combined with heavy rescue equipment can challenge your communication skills.

Make constant eye contact with the other officers at the scene who may have additional information for you about any change in the scene itself. Constantly assess the overall collision area every few minutes and evaluate the need for any changes in your containment.

DRIVER CONTACTS

Once the scene of the collision appears to be somewhat contained, make contact with the drivers and check the potential for any injuries. Drivers who have visible injuries will be helped by the rescue personnel when they arrive shortly at the scene. The drivers who have a *"complaint of pain"* should be asked if they need to be seen by the fire rescue paramedic unit. You should keep the paramedics responding to the scene if either of the parties has a *complaint of pain*. This could help protect you from later potential liability if one or both parties claim you *"canceled the paramedics."*

Often one of the most frustrating occurrences in a major traffic collision can be waiting for the paramedics to arrive. We have all at times felt helpless while waiting those few minutes for the rescue personnel to arrive. The injuries sustained in a collision can be massive and sometimes deceiving. Kindhearted officers in the past have tried to physically help the victims in a collision. This decision can become a *two edged sword* based on today's *civil liability*. Your decision to move an injured victim may later be blamed for compounding the party's injuries. Each decision must be reached on its own merit. Occasionally we must move victims to save their lives from imminent disaster if they were to remain in the vehicles until the rescue personnel arrive. My best recommendation is to leave the victims in their original positions and try to give them constant verbal assurance and encouragement until properly trained personnel are present.

A major injury traffic collision can greatly compound your ability to gain the needed information to complete your collision report. From experience, the best time to gain this information is after the patient has been stabilized in the ambulance. The fire and rescue personnel will need to be given priority and cooperation in their life saving efforts. Many times the number of fire department rescue personnel around the patient is so overwhelming; you will be forced to wait until the victims have been extracted from the vehicles. Take this opportunity to gain those ever so important witness statements.

WITNESS STATEMENTS

Witness contacts at the scene can be one of the most important factors in your final analysis of how the collision occurred. These witnesses can sometimes quickly disappear from the scene. The rescue personnel will start extracting the victims from the vehicle that may give you the opportunity to make these contacts. Make quick but non aggressive announcements, *"Did anyone see this traffic collision?"* Another, more creative approach could be something like, *"Did anyone see what happened in this poor tragic incident?"* The important point is to gain the willing assistance of a disinterested witness.

During this contact, sound empathetic towards the collision and the witnesses' willingness to get involved and remain at the scene. If the collision takes place in the morning or evening *"rush hours"*, you may offer a courtesy notification by phone to the witness's place of employment or home. This may make a witness more comfortable and they may not feel the pressure to leave the scene. If the witness states he or she must leave, ask for a phone number where they can be reached at a time when an interview can be conducted. This will allow the witness to continue to their destination, and you will still be provided with a much needed and important insight into what took place. By gaining a phone number, you will be able to ask questions which may not yet have occurred to you at the scene.

EVIDENCE

Evidence can be collected during the investigation or once the scene is cleared. Collision related evidence can quickly disappear and be influenced by many factors. One of the essential rules in evidence collection is to protect the evidence from any outside contamination. While walking the scene, be sure to check for any trace evidence that will become important to your investigation. The purpose of the collision investigation is to *"find out what occurred."* The vehicles, for example, must be placed at the scene and in the same collision. This may sound basic, but damage must be consistent with what the witnesses, drivers, passengers, and evidence tells you. Any of these factors which is not supportive of the others may be a tell tale sign of either a *staged collision* or a mistaken analysis by the investigator. A combination of all of these factors will lead you to a conclusion of how the collision occurred.

Check for evidence of the *A.O.I.* or any information that might assist you in determining where the collision occurred on the roadway surface. Evidence at the scene is often ignored by investigators. Officers tend to be rushed to a quick determination of the *primary collision factor* and lose sight of how to support their respective conclusion. A skidmark left at the scene may be just the right piece of evidence in a later examination by a qualified Collision Reconstructionist. This skid analysis may support a driver's claim he or she was not exceeding the speed limit as accused by a party found most at fault. Evidence collection and interpretation will be discussed more thoroughly in the following chapters.

HAZARDOUS MATERIALS

Hazardous materials are on the move around us every day. They are transported by commercial vehicles, trains, and by businesses in limited and restricted amounts. These vehicles traverse the same highways most of us travel each day. The general public does not pay much attention to these transportation vehicles until there is a collision where the potential for injury is eminent. Vehicles that transport these chemicals, explosives, and liquid propellants are involved in collisions every year. The majority of these incidents come to a safe conclusion due to the manner in which the collision scene was managed.

There is a great deal of material available on the use and handling of hazardous materials. We will attempt to only scratch the surface of the information available on hazardous materials incidents. Your agency should maintain a *manual* that gives specific direction in the way these incidents are handled. The Fontana Police Department employs a civilian *Emergency Services Specialist.* He is a ready resource for questions and provides our department with outside departmental contacts in cases where hazardous material incidents occur within the city limits.

The list below will be a set of possible considerations which you may choose to utilize when encountering hazardous materials in your *scene management.* You may use this checklist as a guide, but it is recommended that you check with your respective departments to verify if a specific *emergency plan* exists which addresses this type of situation.

First responders checklist

1. Confirm, if possible, if *hazardous materials* are suspected to be involved.
2. Approach from *upwind* if at all possible.
3. Try to *identify* the material if a *hazardous material placard* is visible.
4. Other means may also be available to identify the shipment, *e.g. product name, carrier name, and the container shape.*
5. *Communicate* your views to the dispatcher or your immediate supervisor.
6. Is the substance *leaking* or *spilling?*
7. Consider *evacuation* and the amount of personnel needed to accomplish this task.

8. Approach *cautiously* using only proper protection gear.

9. If you observe a *fire*, withdraw to a safe distance.

HAZARDOUS MATERIALS CONFIRMATION

The first few minutes you arrive on the scene can be the most critical. *"The first responders"* decisions can be crucial to the safety of the parties involved and to the general public at large. Witnesses may provide your dispatch center with information regarding a spill before you arrive at the scene. If this is the case, be prepared to take charge of the scene until the fire department personnel arrive.

HOW DO I APPROACH THE SCENE?

The answer to this question is not difficult as you can imagine. The general rule is to approach from *upwind* if at all possible. Many of today's hazardous materials will be colorless and even odorless. The best way to confirm your suspicions would be to use binoculars from a distance. A safe approach will most likely be accomplished by properly trained fire department personnel.

MATERIAL IDENTIFICATION

The product in the container may be difficult of not nearly impossible to identify. Hazardous materials are regulated by *The Department of Transportation* and must meet set standards for both handling and packaging. The *shape of the container, manufacturer's name, product name, placard ID, or shipping papers will be the most likely source of identifying the spill.*

COMMUNICATIONS

You are the eyes and the ears of the responding units. The fire personnel will look for the preliminary information you have gained as a source for evaluating their approach to the scene. Advise the other responding units of the *exact location of the incident, the wind direction, and safe avenue of approach.* Use your binoculars if approaching the scene is not practical. The shift supervisor will be making tactical plans for handling the incident while enroute to your location.

LEAKS OR SPILLS

Leaks and spills are especially possible in traffic collisions that involve other vehicles besides the transporting vehicle itself. This increases the potential hazard to those persons who frequent collision scenes *e.g.* witnesses, interested persons, and near-by residents. Depending on the type and nature of the spilled substance (gasoline or an explosive), immediate evacuation may be necessary.

SPECIALISTS

Once the fire department arrives on scene, the chances are they will be calling a special *hazardous materials team.* These emergency personnel have been highly trained in the handling and disposal of these materials. They will have the proper equipment to make a safe approach to the scene. The police department's role will most likely be limited to the task of scene containment and possible evacuation control if this is deemed necessary. Your shift supervisor will be making periodic decisions in concert with the actions of the fire department.

RECONSTRUCTION TEAM NOTIFICATION

Cities and counties have seen an increase in the lawsuits filed by victims of traffic collisions. The parties involved in collisions and their respective attorneys are pointing toward faulty roadway design, poor lighting and other various reasons why they were involved in the collision. Because of this, agencies are beginning to look for ways to fight this ever-increasing area of civil litigation. Traffic enforcement has not always been as specialized as it is today. Traffic officers were selected to enforce the vehicle code and investigate the collisions that occur day to day in their cities. Many times, they did not receive the formal training necessary to determine the cause of the more complex collision. Officers placed in traffic positions may have the desire to further their education, but their departments may lack the resources to accomplish this task. For this reason, traffic officers may be faced with very complex collisions that will test their abilities to come to a fair and accurate conclusion.

Traffic investigation has always been somewhat specialized, but the training available focuses much more on the dynamics of the collision rather than civil protection of the entity which employs the specialist. Officers today armed with proper training and experience can virtually explain the mathematical aspects of why the collision occurred.

Due to the severity of a collision, a more trained investigator may be required to perform the investigation.

Each department may take a different approach to the importance of collision investigation. Depending on manpower, some departments may not elect to have a traffic unit at all. Major collisions would be investigated by a neighboring department or the California Highway Patrol. If your department does not have a *reconstruction team* but is moving toward assembling one, consider these important factors: One properly investigated traffic collision could pay for the *reconstruction unit* with the money saved by not having to defend itself in a *potential lawsuit.* Administrators have often been heard to say, *"How often do we really get sued in a collision case?"* This would be very hard to answer unless the plaintiff's attorney was to contact your department after deciding *against* a civil lawsuit.

Reconstructing a collision is not always necessary. Each case must be evaluated on its own merit. The potential for civil liability to the city or county in which you work should be the paramount factor in this decision. A trained Reconstructionist can make an evaluation of the incident and recommend a course of action based on his or her training. The responding field officers remaining at the scene will assist and potentially gain valuable experience from participating in a traffic collision investigation of this caliber. The goal of any reconstruction team should be to remain professional, fair in their investigation and provide support to the field officers relieving them from handling the collision themselves.

Most departments are under the pressure of a fixed budget and may be concerned about the cost of the *overtime*. The supervisor on the scene must weigh all of these factors and make a decision that is right for your department's individual needs. If you face a situation that may become a *reconstruction team call-out*, consider taking the following steps:

- *Contact your respective supervisor* and *explain your concerns*. You will have the best insight into the reason the incident should be investigated in this manner.
- *Freeze the scene* including all vehicles and evidence present. This would include utilizing crime scene tape if available. These steps will help limit the number of interested parties who may contaminate your scene.
- *Limit* the amount of police personnel into and out of the collision scene. Treat the scene in the same manner as you would a crime scene. Check the positioning of the police vehicles and confirm they have not have driven over or parked on any potential physical evidence.
- *Be ready to explain* your involvement in the incident and walk through the scene with the collision investigator once he or she arrives. The collision reconstructionist may ask you to explain what was done prior to his or her arrival. Physical evidence on the roadway and in the vehicles will be crucial to the investigation. The team will then take control of the scene and the investigation.

SCENE CLEAN-UP

The scene has been stabilized and the majority of your investigation has been completed. The clean-up process can now begin. The tow-trucks which first had responded are now standing by and ready to tow the involved vehicles. Before removing the vehicles, take one final walk through the collision scene. Evidence that was not visible on your initial evaluation may now appear after the emergency vehicles begin to withdraw from the scene. The lighting conditions may also have changed at this time in the investigation that may help you in locating missing evidence. Skidmarks, that were hidden by emergency vehicles, may be destroyed by leaking vehicle fluids when the tow-trucks begin to move them. Disassemble the scene slowly and look for this disguised evidence.

A secondary set of photographs from these newly gained vantage points may be beneficial to your case. Once the vehicles have been towed and separated, check for evidence which may not have been accessible due to the damage sustained by the vehicles. Follow-up with the tow-truck drivers and ensure they will be sweeping the scene of any debris left behind by the involved vehicles. Leaking fluids can be extremely slippery to both pedestrians and passing motorists. Glass debris from headlights and safety windows should be swept by the tow drivers before they leave the scene. Fluids should either be *washed down* or *cleaned using absorbent,* e.g. *sand or dirt.* The agency investigating and controlling the scene is responsible for ensuring the roadway is safe for travel before any other vehicles are allowed to traverse the roadway.

Take a final look around the scene after all vehicles and debris has been swept and cleaned-up. Check for any traffic control signs that will need to be replaced to make the roadway safe for passing motorists. Your city or county yards' agencies are an excellent source for portable stop signs and signal maintenance. Minor repair items such as street name marking signs, overhead lighting and some less than essential traffic control signs will be left to the discretion of the officer or supervisor on the scene.

THIS PAGE INTENTIONALLY LEFT BLANK

4

PHOTOGRAPHY

PHOTOGRAPHY

Webster's New World Dictionary defines photography as *"The art or process of producing pictorial images on a surface sensitive to light or other radiant energy, as on film in a camera."* Police officers and investigators alike often take photos to reproduce a collision scene for later examination. These photographs can support conclusions as well as refresh the investigator's memory a number of years after the incident. They also serve to prevent civil litigation after the location has been altered.

Daily, officers take photos of evidence they deem necessary in a criminal investigation. These photos are later reviewed by detectives, attorneys, and sometimes even the media. Most officers receive limited formal training in the basic academy of *what is important* when assessing the need for photographs. The officer rarely receives instruction as to the proper framing techniques which present the most favorable representation of the subject matter. Never has this been so important as to the accident investigator.

The accident investigator has a responsibility to produce a well documented and supported decision about the cause of the accident. This decision is made by examination of the evidence at the scene, statements, damage of the vehicles, and a number of other possible factors. Photographs can support your overall conclusions of how the accident occurred. Most, if not all police departments, provide film and cameras upon request for its officers. Each department will have informal, if not formal guidelines regarding which accident investigations will be photographed by its officers. Contact your departmental supervision for clarification of this issue.

Several departments have modified their investigative procedures in the handling and documentation of accident investigations. Many California police departments have stopped investigating all but the most serious injury accidents. Each incident must be evaluated on its own merit with respect to photographs. Make a clear assessment of the potential liability to the city or county in which you are employed. The accident investigator is charged with the responsibility of protecting the city or county against any litigation which may surface later. Photographs may settle a dispute many years after the collision investigation has been completed.

WHAT TO LOOK FOR AT THE SCENE

Once you arrive at the scene, make a quick fast walk through of the entire area. This should include all vehicles present and any potential visible evidence. Depending on the severity of the collision, other officers may be there to assist you. With experience, you will make a speedy preliminary decision as to what might have occurred. Take a few seconds to *slow the incident down* and ask *"Are photos necessary in this case?"* If the answer is *yes*, begin assigning priority to those personnel that will be *freezing the scene* for you. Many departments assign a single traffic officer to investigate the entire collision. Ask for additional assistance if manpower is an immediate issue in preserving the scene. *"Freezing the scene"* may become a major challenge to many officers. Pressure can manifest itself in a variety of forms. Area traffic, supervision, and scene containment can all have a tremendous impact in the rush to clear the roadway.

The scene itself may play a role in your decision making process. Fire department, paramedic and police personnel can all contaminate the scene with their equipment. Arriving emergency personnel often park their vehicles in very close proximity to the accident scene. Large emergency vehicles can make your job that much more difficult. The rotating emergency lights and strobes can greatly alter your ability to *frame the scene* properly. The equipment itself can block the entire accident area.

Those involved in the collision investigation and the parties themselves can sometime block your camera position

The time of day and weather can also dramatically change the conditions of the roadway. The wind, rain, snow and lighting changes may misrepresent what you originally observed at the time of your walk-through. Can the evidence be observed clearly? This may sound like a great deal to remember amongst other investigative facts, but the decision will need to be made quickly utilizing these factors.

EQUIPMENT

A variety of photography equipment is available on the market today. The majority of officers in the field now carry a Polaroid® camera with departmental issued film. Other departments issue 35mm cameras to officers in the field. Cameras are also made available to officers upon request of a supervisor. *Time is of the essence at a collision scene*, and therefore the request for a camera should be made early in the first few minutes of your investigation. A combination of 35mm and Polaroid® photography is the safest for the majority of your applications. The 35mm photos will be the clearest representation of the scene. The Polaroid® photos can become a good security measure against a roll of lost or misplaced 35mm film. These photos will refresh your memory while making those sometimes complicated decisions about what caused the collision.

Consider assembling a photo kit that will expedite your response to the collision scene. This kit can be fully stocked with a small compact 35mm camera, many rolls of film, and a Polaroid® camera. Check the kit regularly for battery freshness and film usage. A video camera may serve as a *witness to the magnitude of the collision.* The Fontana Police Department, for example, has purchased a traffic D.U.I. trailer with a grant from *The Office of Traffic Safety.* This trailer is fully stocked with reflective traffic cones, overhead lighting, and storage compartments. My personal camera and all relative equipment is stored in a locked container in this trailer for ready access in the event of a major incident.

Police agencies in the 90's are concerned with the budget crunch. This may have an adverse affect in your efforts to obtain photo equipment and film from your department. Equipment may also be assembled from confiscated property found in the evidence sections of your respective departments. Evidence and property not claimed by the owners may be sent to *auction* and will be an outstanding source for some very nice equipment. The 35mm camera, Polaroid® camera, and video camera currently in use by my department were obtained in this manner. Contact your department's property clerk and inquire about this method of assembling equipment

WHAT PHOTOS SHOULD I TAKE?

Each collision scene must be evaluated for the correct number of photos. The following is a suggested priority list; however, you may choose to adjust the order in which these photos are taken due to unforeseen changes in evidence disposition at the collision scene.

Involved vehicles

1. All vehicles involved in the collision and their current positions.
2. Any significant damage which may substantiate the dynamics of the collision.

3. The area of impact, if located, which would support the vehicles' *post* impact directions.
4. Lighting or turn signal indicators (interior) and current positions of each at the time of your investigation.
5. Seat belt positions and their current condition, if applicable.

Scene

1. Photos of the scene both from a distance and from all relative directions of travel.
2. Relevant traffic control signs and signals. This would include speed limit signs, roadway markings, and *"warning ahead"* signs.

Fatalities

1. Position of the body inside or out of the vehicle.
2. Potential injury locations on the vehicle identified by body fluids or tissue residue.
3. Close examination photos of the injury, if possible, once permission is gained from the coroner.
4. All clothing removed from the body at the time of your investigation.
5. Any clothing items separated from the victim's body by the impact.
6. Facial photos of the victim if identity of the party is not known.

COLLISIONS WHICH DON'T FIT THESE GUIDELINES

Occasionally you will respond to a collision that challenges your photographic abilities. Each collision presents a different hurdle in taking the right photos. The guidelines listed above will assist you in the majority of the accidents you investigate. You may however investigate a commercial truck, train, or bicycle collision that will require additional photographs. Your investigative needs will help determine what items will become important later. Apply the above guidelines whenever possible when considering these factors.

The commercial trucking industry often carries heavy loads that may have a dramatic effect on the braking systems of the vehicles they drive. Use the same inspection process for your photographs as you would in the collision analysis itself. A train accident, for example, will have a large *explosive impact* and can spread debris and destruction over a large area. Bicycle accident photos may be limited to the brakes and handle bar area of the frame. Divide the collision data into a list of the impact locations and inspection information. This information can be applied to a variety of crashes merely by changing the involved vehicles noted on the list above.

PHOTOGRAPHER POSITIONING

We have all taken photos of our families, friends, and vacations using a wide variety of photo equipment. The photos taken in a collision investigation must reflect the point of view you are trying to present. The stance, height, and location of your photos can dramatically change the viewer's perspective of the accident scene. Once you have made your choice of the subject matter, consider how the photo will match the narrative description in your report.

Start with the vehicles involved in the collision and work outward to the perimeter of the collision scene. Select the vehicle that you have determined to be the *party who contributed most to the impact.* Take a minimum of *eight photos* of each vehicle involved. This standard applies to the average passenger vehicle or truck and can be expanded if necessary. The following will be an example of the *eight photos* and the appropriate angles from which they should be taken.

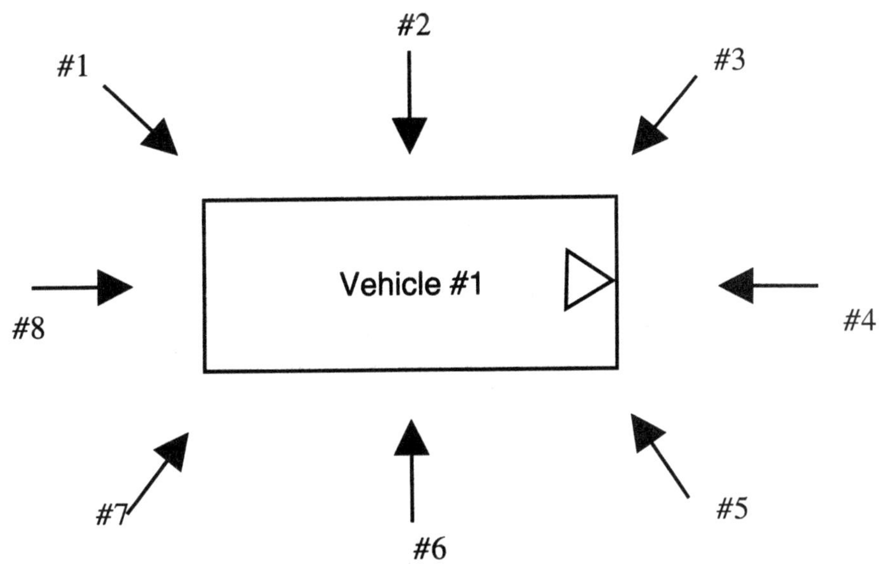

Take the intended photograph from a distance to correlate the evidence to a specific vehicle or area of the scene. This will give the viewers a reference point in the scene as they work through the pictures as a whole. Once this has been completed, move much closer and zoom into the subject matter (evidence) and take a detailed photo. When you have taken photos from these angles expand and concentrate your efforts toward the area of the most significant damage. Frame the area of impact and shoot your picture. If necessary, you can zoom into the area for a close-up. The close-up photos can play a very important role in helping the investigator determine the location of paint transfers, debris directions, or sheer damage to the vehicles. The earlier suggested interior photographs can be taken after you have completed the preliminary exterior shots of the vehicle. Experiment and test your photography skills. You will quickly gain experience and learn what works best in certain situations.

Take a photo of the vehicles from a short distance away to highlight their positions at the scene.

LIGHTING CONDITIONS

Lighting conditions can play a very important role in the clarity and sharpness of your photographs. Lighting can shift and change during your investigation sometimes greatly limiting your ability to frame the appropriate intended damage or evidence. Afternoon shadows or overhead street lighting can cause the photo to be blocked or over-exposed. A daylight shot of a vehicle may require the use of an external flash unit to fill the area and make it visible. Some of today's more modern cameras are equipped with a *"fill flash"* unit. Check your camera equipment and familiarize yourself with the features of the flash attachment. Take a few seconds and check the visibility of the evidence frequently during the course of the investigation.

Sometimes a skidmark that was not visible when you arrived may suddenly and without warning become visible as the sun rises or sets. Place a reference card or measuring device in the photo if at all possible on all of your close-up shots. The true view of the intended object can be distorted in a closely shot photograph. A measuring tape will give the evidence a more realistic size and appearance when being evaluated at a later time.

Use a measuring tape or reference card in your close-up photos to identify their size whenever possible.

Lighting or lack of lighting should be assessed when selecting an external flash unit. The most desirable unit will have a distance sensor allowing a *"hands free"* adjustment of the lighting directed at the intended target area. This type of feature will speed the unit's recharge and usage time allowing you more time to plan your next shot. If you are forced to use a manual flash unit, ensure the *ASA* (film speed) and distance settings are correct for the flash and camera.

Once the photos have been taken and collected, the scene can never be completely duplicated. Consider using portable lighting in your overall scene photography. Most of today's flash units are not powerful enough to project light the required distance to depict your point of view. Overhead lighting utilized by fire departments or D.U.I. trailers can be directed into the scene. Many departments utilize ID technicians in major traffic collision investigations. Many of these ID technicians have experience in *"painting with light."* For those not familiar with this technique, a flashlight is used with an *open and exposed* lens allowing the scene to take on a daylight appearance. Don't forget to take a few *"natural lighting"* shots not assisted by flash units if the lighting played a major role in the collision.

EXTERIOR SCENE PHOTOGRAPHS

After completing all of your vehicle injury/fatal and other interior evidence shots, you may move onto the overall scene photos. Repeat the photo positions used on the vehicles for the full scene. Stand in the same *"eight"* positions, only from a much broader base. Each time you complete your shots, assess the need for a more expanded shot at a greater distance. Include all signs, signals, crosswalks, warning signs, and street lighting that may prove to be important at a later date. For instance, a speed sign may be a very significant factor in the collision. A speed survey may change the posted speed limit on the street at a later time, and therefore the original sign will have been replaced.

Adding exterior photos to your evidence collection can protect your city from a claim of poor roadway design or the lack of proper signage.

FOLLOW-UP INVESTIGATION

Once the investigation has been completed at the scene, you may choose to inspect the vehicles on the flatbed transport tow trailers. This may provide you with a secondary opportunity to view the vehicles undercarriage and frame. Any other important follow-up investigation should be documented with the use of additional photographs. A visit to the tow company yards may prove to be fruitful in your quest to solve a more complicated accident puzzle. The vehicles may be placed back together in the original pre-impact positions that will give the investigator an inside view into the principal *direction of force*. This *"jigsaw"* vehicle placement can have a dramatic effect in your presentation to a deputy district attorney or jury. The vehicles can be repositioned in their natural crash positions at a tow yard or vacant parking lot.

Once the vehicles have been fitted together, stretch yellow evidence tape over the main axis of each vehicle indicating the vehicle's original direction of travel. The tape will assist you in visualizing how the vehicles contacted one another. The tape should be extended over the trunk, hood, and roof toward the other impacting vehicle. Contact your local fire department and ask for their assistance. They will provide you with a long ladder or crane. This will allow you to climb above the vehicles. Elevate yourself above the vehicles to take several photos of the damage and approach angles of the involved vehicles.

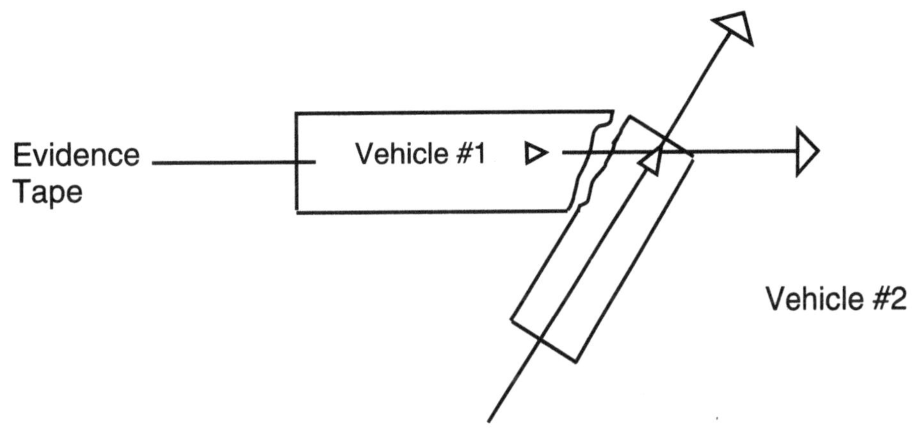

AERIAL PHOTOGRAPHY

Aerial photography can be a great tool when the case is presented to the district attorney. Photos from the air can clearly and accurately depict the roadway, painted lane dividers, painted approach warnings and speeds for the area. Roadway signs and markings can often fade or change as the years go by. How the roadway looked on the day or evening of the collision can be very important in civil proceeding against the city or county. Overhead signals and street lights may be visible from the air and can possibly *"put to rest"* a complaint of possible design or engineering errors.

Contact your local aviation division or Sheriff's Department and talk with them about a possible *"photo flight"* of an intersection which would be considered valuable evidence in your case. Most pilots and observers have experience in this area and possibly have provided this service on earlier occasions to your Investigation and Narcotic's Divisions. Have your camera and film ready before departing. If at all possible, brief the pilot and observer about the collision itself and any relevant photo angles that would best facilitate your needs.

Try to use the same *eight photos* discussed earlier in this chapter and apply them to the air. Take *four photos* from each direction looking toward the intersection where the accident took place. Use a telephoto lens and frame the scene in a manner to best represent the roadway markings from the air. From experience, the best shots appear to be taken from directly over the intersection looking down. The observer will remove the rear door for you upon request that will make your shot much clearer. The helicopter's Plexiglas® windows can sometimes distort the images.

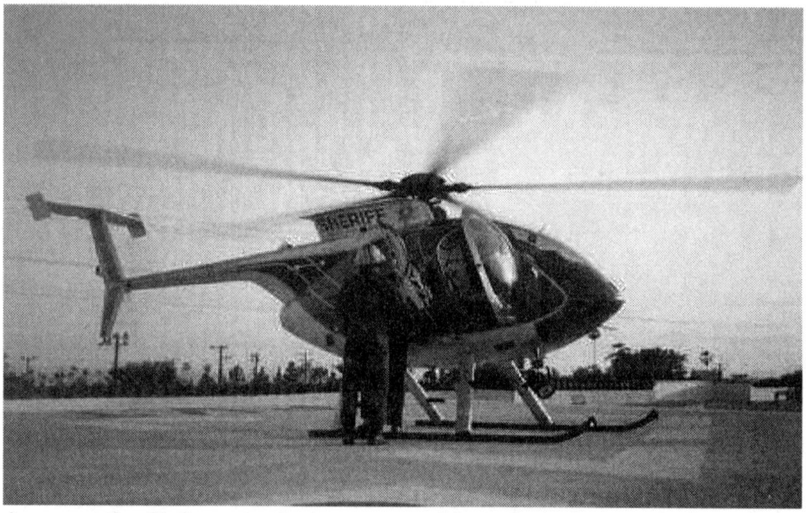

Use your city or counties Air Support unit whenever possible to obtain photographs from above the scene.

The best time to take aerial photos is directly after the collision and before the scene is cleared. This is not always practical, and therefore the following day is acceptable. The vehicle positions will still be marked in place at the scene and will provide a more truly accurate view of the debris, direction of travel, and magnitude of the collision. The roadway paint will also be visible at this time. Traffic congestion on the roadway must be taken into consideration and can block the area where the collision occurred. A patrol officer placed in the proper location can quickly close the road for the short time the photos are being taken.

EVIDENCE & PHOTO MARKINGS

Be sure to mark all of your rolls of film as they are used. Keep several rolls of film in your collision investigation kit. Apply a piece of masking tape to each roll and mark the case number on it as the film is loaded into the camera. This will save some time and confusion when the film is placed into evidence or is possibly misplaced in the police vehicle. Total the photographs at the scene and place the film into an evidence bag. Log the aerial photos separately, for quick reference. Complete your evidence sheets at the station and be sure to book all evidence into the lockers immediately after your return from the scene.

5

THE VEHICLE CODE

INTRODUCTION

California has one of the World's most complex driving environments. Many of the highways and freeways within major California cities present a difficult challenge to the average driver. The state's 16 million plus drivers and 20 million plus vehicles far exceeds the total of any other state and most foreign countries. The many signs, lights, and traffic patterns have been designed to promote the *smooth flow of traffic*. The California Vehicle Code, first *enacted in 1905*, is an accumulation of laws that regulate the use of motor vehicles on California highways. The public at large, however, does not fully understand the vehicle code. The majority of drivers have never read the vehicle code and therefore are not very educated as to the *rules of the road.*

The vehicle code is available in various formats from LawTech. The *QWIK-CODE* primarily contains the enforcement sections in summary form. The *Abridged* version contains the same sections that are in the *QWIK-CODE*, but in their full text format. The *Unabridged* version contains the full text of all the Vehicle Code sections. They are updated annually to include all new legislative changes and are available in print or on disk the first week or two of each year.

LEGISLATIVE CHANGES

The *QWIK-CODE* version illustrates legislative changes with a note at the end of the section which explains what the change encompasses. In the versions of the Vehicle Code which include the full text of the sections, legislative amendments are indicated with underlining for the new text and asterisks where text was deleted. Newly added sections are indicated with a footnote indicating the year it was added.

CATEGORIES AND SECTIONS

Statutes fall within *four* categories according to their content. Each "Section" (*i.e.* statute) must be carefully read as it may fall within one or more of these categories. Only *Punitive* sections may be cited.

(A) **Definitive Sections:** (***May not cite***)

These sections *define*, *limit*, or *explain* the meaning of the words or phrases.

(B) **Procedural Sections:** (***May not cite***)

These sections describe the method of proceeding in a course of action or provide *rules of law* by which legal actions are conducted. Such statutes state the proper method to follow without requiring punishment for failure to comply.

(C) **Authoritative Sections:** (***May not cite***)

These sections *grant authority* to individuals or entities.

(D) **Punitive Sections:** (***May cite***)

These sections require or prohibit certain action and usually provide a *prescribed punishment* or *penalty* for the violations that were committed. Acts committed or omitted are in violation of the law and the violator *may be cited.* Such acts are classified as *Felonies, Misdemeanors, or Infractions*.

LIST OF VIOLATIONS

A list of violations (*punitive sections*), in order of code section numbers, appears in the rear of the vehicle code published by D.M.V., and in the *QWIK-CODE* published by LawTech. The *QWIK-CODE* also includes a summary of each section, plus other non-punitive related sections for a clearer understanding of the enforcement sections. Both of the above titles indicate just prior to the section number an *I* for *infractions*, an *M* for *misdemeanors*, and a *F* for *felonies*. The *QWIK-CODE* also indicates a *C* for sections considered as civil only and includes other handy field reference information. (*See back cover for QWIK-CODE ordering information.*)

THE VEHICLE CODE AS A SOURCE

It is recommended that you review the most often used sections that will become important in collision investigations. The vehicle code contains numerous references as well as definitions of such items as *"What constitutes a residential or commercial area"* or *"What are the hours of darkness"* etc. Each accident investigator should possess a good working knowledge of the vehicle code or be able to locate the appropriate section to clarify the code's *language*. The vehicle code can a be a source of vast knowledge when discussing traffic enforcement. The rules of the road printed in the code may relieve or impose authority on you during the course of your daily law enforcement activities.

ENFORCEMENT

Traffic accidents result in death, injury, and material losses that add to more than all other matters of police responsibility *combined.* The rules of the road contained in the vehicle code were enacted to promote *smooth* and *rapid flow of traffic* thus reducing conflict. When officers *fail* to enforce traffic laws, accidents tend to increase with resulting fatalities, injuries, and property damage. The efficient flow of traffic is impeded, and *the police image suffers.* Traffic enforcement can be directly correlated to the increase or reduction of traffic accidents in a given area.

Traffic enforcement is not always popular, but very necessary.
The general public expects officers to enforce the traffic laws.

A successful traffic operation can have a major impact on a location with both visibility and liability. Once the officer or department is made aware of a given *problem area,* collisions which follow may become a *"political hot potato."* The high visibility of a traffic enforcement program in a problem area may have a two-fold effect. The complaining residents may be pleased with the service and a traffic collision may be averted.

Traffic enforcement is not always popular, but it is very necessary. The right approach on a traffic stop may have a dramatic affect on the recipient's attitude in receiving the citation. Patient and understanding attitudes present a significant challenge in a traffic enforcement contact. Due to the sheer *volume* of stops a traffic officer may make, he or she is bound to offend a violator simply by the nature of the stop itself. Each officer must learn to balance this enforcement style with the need for the action itself.

AUTHORITY TO CITE AT A COLLISION SCENE

Peace Officers Standards and Training (P.O.S.T.) requires each investigating officer to complete a *Basic Collision Investigation School* before issuing a *"written notice to appear." 40600(a) CVC* provides peace officers with the authority to issue a citation based on the results of a collision investigation. This can become a very unpopular task when undertaken at a collision scene. Investigating officers are often asked at the collision scene to make an *immediate decision* as to what caused the accident. These decisions can lead to arguments and complaints against the investigating officer. The majority of traffic officers have come to the conclusion as to the cause of the crash before they clear the scene; however, they choose not to communicate this to the involved parties.

It is recommended that you do not complete a citation including the *P.C.F.* (Primary Collision Factor) at the scene unless you are very sure the receiving party is ready for this secondary emotional blow. The traffic collision and damage to their respective vehicles can be a very emotional experience. There are reported incidents where officers have been dispatched to calls where the involved parties have been *"fist fighting"* over who caused the collision. In such cases it's advisable to tell the parties your decision will be made after you spend time reviewing the statements and evidence. You may then complete and mail the citation to the party found most at fault.

THE MORE IMPORTANT SECTIONS

The California Vehicle Code contains thousands of individual sections, but only a few will carry a great deal of weight in a major collision investigation. The majority of the accidents occurring on the roadway today will be an *Infraction* type vehicle code violation. These primary collision factors will either be cited at the scene or after the report is completed. The more serious offenses, such as *Vehicular Manslaughter*, will require a series of facts that prove the driver was *grossly negligent* in his or her operation of the vehicle that caused the collision.

Take the time to review and read the vehicle code whenever possible. No officer is expected to know the code inside and out, but being able to find the appropriate section is half the battle. The California Penal Code also has several chargeable offenses in cases where loss of life occurs. Each of these books will provide you with the proper authority when making recommendations in your collision investigations.

PURSUITS AND THE VEHICLE CODE

Everyday somewhere in the United States, a police officer is involved in a vehicle pursuit. Most end with the capture of the suspect and with no property damage to anyone not involved in the pursuit. Some of these pursuits, however, end in serious traffic collisions and even death. This of course is followed by lawsuits which focus on the reason for the pursuit and if the officer was driving with *due regard* for the safety of the public at large. The California Vehicle Code provides safeguards that may protect you while operating under these above stated guidelines.

Pursuits can be unpredictable and occur rather quickly. But the outcome can be different than what you expected.

Section *21055 CVC* provides an exemption for the officer, fireman, or rescue ambulance personnel responding to an emergency. The emergency vehicle must follow the rules of emergency vehicle operation, and the driver also must be driving with due regard for the public's safety. Most of you are familiar with code three operation which is detailed in the vehicle code. Following rules such as *passing only on the left*, is one of the essential requirements of the vehicle code when driving "*code three.*" Passing on the *right,* for instance, can lead to a traffic collision where you will not be protected by the vehicle code. In the case described above, the general driving public is required to *pull to the right and stop* per *21806(a) CVC*. A collision as a result of this type of scenario would be determined to be the fault of the emergency vehicle operator who is required to *pass on the left.*

Occasionally late in the evening or early morning, we have all observed fire and ambulance vehicles responding to emergencies. The operators sometimes neglect to activate the vehicle's siren instead utilizing only the rotating emergency lights. This simple intentional or unintentional mistake will become a key factor in a collision investigation. In addition, many officers have *"punched'* intersections in order to cut their response times on emergency calls which do not qualify in their departments code three guidelines. The forward red and blue lights are illuminated, but they fail to activate the siren. This vehicle code violation on the part of the emergency vehicle operator would be listed as an associated factor in the collision investigation, should a collision occur.

If a "*code three*" response is authorized, activate your vehicle's siren and rotating emergency lights. Many city and county dispatch centers are now reviewing radio tapes in pursuits that end in a traffic collision. These tapes can play a vital part in supporting the officer's statement that his or her siren was activated. Many times the siren itself can be heard on the radio tapes. These steps can help to protect you in a lawsuit that is almost surely to follow a collision involving a pursuit.

The vehicle code provides civil protection in a potential lawsuit resulting from a collision while responding "*code three.*" The driver of the involved vehicle must be driving in a *reasonable and prudent manner* with *due regard* for the safety of the general public. The emergency vehicle must be operating in a authorized *"code three"* response. Section *CVC 17004* also sometimes referred to as the *"fireman's rule"* provides protection from civil liability if these requirements have been met. This umbrella of protection does not protect you while in the *"non-code three"* mode of operation.

This case law was tested in civil court by a fireman who was returning to his fire station after an emergency run. The truck's emergency lights were *off*, and the vehicle was not authorized to operate in a *"code three"* mode. The driver of the truck was involved in a minor injury traffic collision. The injured party pursued civil damage assessments against the driver and his agency. The fireman claimed he was protected under *CVC 17004* and was not subject to civil liability. The court disagreed and stated the driver did not meet the requirements of this section and was not:

- *Operating his vehicle in a "code three" lights and siren mode of operation.*
- *Responding to an emergency call for service.*

Emergency vehicle collisions can be one of the more difficult accidents to investigate.

Not often will you have the opportunity to investigate an emergency vehicle collision. The majority of these accidents will be investigated by a neutral agency. If you do investigate this type of collision, your agency is looking for the cause of the collision regardless of how *unpopular it may seem.* Most officers involved in a vehicle pursuit fully realize the risks. If a collision occurs at their own hands, they will most likely be honest with you about what caused the accident.

Vehicle pursuits have become a source of many lawsuits, and therefore agencies have taken a major interest in the question *"was the pursuit really necessary?"* Your investigation may play only a limited part in the totality of this question. Your participation may be limited to investigating the cause, checking compliance with the vehicle code, and interviewing any potential witnesses to the collision. If you have been placed in this position, try to take a professional interest only. The staff of your department may have reached its own conclusion well before you have turned in the report. Complete the report in a timely fashion and let the cause of the accident speak for itself.

THIS PAGE INTENTIONALLY LEFT BLANK

6

PRIMARY COLLISION FACTOR

WHAT IS A PRIMARY COLLISION FACTOR?

The *C.I.M.* describes the *primary collision factor* as the *"One element or driving action which in the officer's opinion best describes the primary or main cause of the collision."* The acronym *P.C.F.* is often used in place of the longer phrase. This portion of the collision investigation is extremely important. Many actions can combine together to cause a traffic collision; however only *one* event usually precedes the incident. The investigating officer must make use of all the available information at the scene. A majority of the traffic collisions occur on the public roadways and therefore the California Vehicle Code applies when explaining the *P.C.F.* Occasionally traffic accidents occur on private property. These private property collisions present a special challenge for the investigator. The clear rules of the vehicle code do not apply on private property; however, you are still obligated to make a determination of what caused the collision.

Several independent driving factors may combine together to cause the traffic collision. For example, alcohol may be considered the primary collision factor by itself due to the nature of the offense. Falling asleep at the wheel may also qualify as a *P.C.F.* if the driving action can be substantiated by evidence or a disinterested witness. Many times the primary collision factor cannot be determined from the information available at the scene. This chapter will address these many questions regarding the *choice and determination of the P.C.F.*

DECISIONS, DECISIONS

Many times what appears to be the most simple type of collision can be the most difficult to solve in relation to determining a *primary collision factor*. Take, for example, two drivers who *stop for a stop sign,* then enter the intersection and collide with one another. No independent witness is present at the scene, and both of the drivers claim to *"have the right-of-way."* Collisions do exist where the cause cannot be determined at the scene, or for that matter, at all. Those drivers that appear to have clearly violated the vehicle code and caused the collision will be the easiest to solve. In the case detailed above, the cause of the collision would be *"unknown"* quite simply because the collision occurred, but neither of the parties can be placed as the person who did not stop for the stop sign. One or both may have stopped and simply believed he/she had the right-of-way. A thorough explanation of the circumstances of your decision should be explained in the narrative of the report.

You will investigate many collisions where the cause can be determined, but assigning fault to a specific party is not easy. Each officer must be comfortable in his or her decision of the *P.C.F.* The *C.I.M.* recommends a *P.C.F.* be determined if at all possible. Other available causes of *"unknown, fell asleep, or other"* should not be chosen simply when the officer is unable to locate the appropriate related vehicle code violation. When two or more actions together appear to have caused the accident, choose the vehicle code violation which appears to have *contributed most* to the collision.

VEHICLE CODE SECTION VIOLATIONS

This reference can be found at the back of the C.H.P. 555 form under *"Primary Collision Factor."* This area of the report is where the officer places his or her determination of what caused the collision. The box corresponding to this area must be completed to clarify which of the drivers violated the chosen vehicle code section. The actual vehicle code section should be written or typed underneath this reference. Check the appropriate box with whether the driver was *"cited"* or *"not cited."*

Primary Collision Factors

#1	**A** VC Section Violated ***22106 CVC*** Cited
	B Other Improper driving *
	C Other than Driver *
	D Unknown *
	E Fell Asleep *

Try to be as specific as possible when choosing the vehicle code section that applies to the collision you investigated. This area of the C.H.P. 555 is only used for those collisions that occur on the public roadways. The only exception to this general rule might be a *dedicated alley* or *incorporated private driveway, e.g. a patrolled street in a mall.* Check with your local engineering departments for the status of these roadways.

A driver who has been involved in a traffic collision, but is also *under the influence* of alcohol or drugs will be one of the exceptions to the standard *P.C.F.* The cause of the accident may have been a red light violation, however the *D.U.I.* (driving under the influence) will be substituted as the *P.C.F.* The red light violation will become the *"other associated factor."* The D.U.I. becomes the primary collision factor in any collision where the D.U.I. driver is found to have caused the collision. On rare occasions, the *D.U.I.* driver is determined *not to have caused the collision.*

This presents an interesting paradox to the investigating officer. The D.U.I. driver did not cause the accident, but could his or her alcohol influence have been a factor in the overall incident? In this scenario the party found most at fault would be listed adjacent to the *"Primary Collision Factor"* category of the report. The *D.U.I.* or *23152 CVC* violation will be added as an *"Other associated factor."* The driver who was under the influence should not have been behind the wheel at all and therefore has a *minor association* in the accident.

When attempting to determine a *primary collision factor* in a major collision scene, consider *ALL* of the possibilities. This may include physical evidence, witness statements, and vehicle damage. Examine the damage to the vehicles and compare this damage to the statements of the involved drivers. We have all been tempted at times to make a *rush decision* when investigating a collision. Taking extra time in selecting an appropriate vehicle code violation and explaining your reasoning in the report may save you embarrassment in a deposition at a later time. In certain circumstances you can determine the *PCF* but not the party *"found most at fault."* In this type of collision, the investigator should place an *"X"* in the box for *"VC Section Violated"* and write the appropriate section adjacent to it.

OTHER IMPROPER DRIVING

This selection under the heading of *"Primary Collision Factor"* may be used when the cause of the collision cannot be determined using the vehicle code. A *Private Property Collision* that does not fall under the jurisdiction of the California Vehicle Code may be described in this area. Place the corresponding party number adjacent to this selection and describe the *"Other Improper Driving."* For example, a driver who was found to have *backed his vehicle in an unsafe manner* and violated *22106 CVC* on a public roadway *could not be cited* for the same violation on private property. The investigating officer would need to complete the C.H.P. 555 face sheet in the following manner:

Primary Collision Factors

	A VC Section Violated Cited
#1	**B** Other Improper driving * ***Unsafe Backing***
	C Other than Driver *
	D Unknown *
	E Fell Asleep *

OTHER THAN DRIVER

This area of the *Primary Collision Factor* should be checked when the cause of the collision was *beyond the driver's control.* The following examples could be considered as justifications for selecting this area of the P.C.F.

1. A *large animal* such as a deer, horse or cow runs into the path of the damaged vehicle.

2. The driver of the involved vehicle has a *heart attack, seizure, or diabetic coma.*

3. The driver of a vehicle that is being operated safely strikes *black ice.*

4. Unforeseen mechanical failure occurs which was not detected during *routine maintenance.* This could include *transmission lock-up or metal fatigue, etc.*

5. A vehicle's tires throw up a rock into the path of another vehicle. If at all possible, this type of information should be corroborated by a disinterested party.

As with all other specific selections not relating to the vehicle code, this should not be used as a catch-all relieving the investigating officer from his/her duty to select a corresponding vehicle code violation better describing the PCF.

Primary Collision Factors

	A VC Section Violated Cited
	B Other Improper driving *
X	**C** Other than Driver *
	D Unknown *
	E Fell Asleep *

Mark an "*X*" adjacent to the section of *"other than driver."* The specific notation of what caused the collision may not appropriately fit into the space provided. For this reason, *explain your selection in the narrative.*

UNKNOWN

Mark an "*X*" in this box and explain the reason for your selection in the body of the report. Many times the cause of the accident cannot be determined due to the lack of information or a disinterested witness who can shed light on the more responsible party at fault. For this reason, no corresponding party number should be placed adjacent to this selection.

Primary Collision Factors

	A VC Section Violated Cited
	B Other Improper driving *
	C Other than Driver *
X	**D** Unknown *
	E Fell Asleep *

FELL ASLEEP

This selection should only be made when the investigating officer can establish the driver who caused the accident *fell asleep*. This can be determined by the driver's statement supported by a potential passenger or some other physical evidence. A driver's statement alone would not ordinarily be enough to satisfy this requirement when the physical evidence conflicts with this claim. If the investigating officer does conclude the driver *fell asleep*, a *possible associated factor* may also be applicable.

Choose the box corresponding to the selection *fell asleep* and indicate which of the drivers will be responsible for this element. The facts supporting your decision in this matter should be explained in detail within the narrative.

Primary Collision Factors

	A VC Section Violated Cited
	B Other Improper driving *
	C Other than Driver *
	D Unknown *
X	**E** Fell Asleep *

OTHER ASSOCIATED FACTORS

This section of the C.H.P. 555 report will assist the investigating officer to explain the possible secondary factor that may have partially contributed to the collision. As stated in the previous pages of this chapter, collisions can be caused by a combination of factors. The most significant of causes will be listed as the *Primary Collision Factor*. Other supporting violations can also have a strong impact in determining the *P.C.F.* however will not be the leading factor. These supporting movements or driving errors are called *"Other Associated Factors."* This referenced area of the accident report can be found on the second page (rear of) the C.H.P. 555. The diagram below is a similar reproduction of this area.

1	2	3	OTHER ASSOCIATED FACTOR(S) *(MARK 1 TO 2 ITEMS)*
			A VC SECTION VIOLATION CITED
			B VC SECTION VIOLATION CITED
			C VC SECTION VIOLATION CITED
			D

Mark an "*X*" in the box which corresponds to the party which you have found contributed in some form to the accident and *list the appropriate vehicle code violation* adjacent to it in the framed area. Once listed, indicate whether the party was *cited*. Several *"Other Associated Factors"* are listed directly below this area which may apply to your determination of what occurred. The C.I.M. allows the investigating officer *two selections* including the one referenced above. The following is a list of these possible selections.

- Vision Obscurement
- Inattention
- Stop and Go Traffic
- Entering/Leaving Ramp
- Previous Collision
- Unfamiliar with Road
- Defective Vehicle Equipment
- Uninvolved Vehicle
- Other
- None Apparent
- Runaway Vehicle

Vision Obscurement

Indicate the type of *Obscurement* and specify how it affected the driver in the accident. Drivers will often claim the *"sun was in my eyes."* This may be a valid obscurement, but a thorough explanation will keep attorneys from questioning a secondary non-moveable obscurement such as tree limbs or construction dust. Mark this element if *"F" or other* under weather is marked.

Inattention

Mark this selection if the investigating officer determines *inattention* was an *associated factor* in the collision. This might apply in a collision where the driver indicates he or she was distracted in some way just before the accident. This should not be used as a catch-all. Explain in the narrative what distraction diverted the attention of the driver possibly contributing to the cause of the collision.

Stop & Go Traffic

This area should be primarily *self-explanatory*, however the investigating officer is encouraged to explain the congestion of the traffic in the area where the collision took place.

Entering/Leaving Ramp

This would apply in a collision where one of the involved drivers states they were entering or leaving an on or off ramp. The on ramp and off ramp may be adjacent to a overpass intersection. The decelerating speed estimate by the party should be explained in your narrative.

Previous Collision

The officer would mark this selection if the collision was a result of possible *congestion* due to an earlier traffic collision and was a factor in the secondary accident. This should be explained in the narrative portion of your report.

Unfamiliar with Road

This area is again somewhat *self-explanatory;* however, the investigating officer is encouraged to explain the driver's statement and why this would be a factor in the collision.

Defective Vehicle Equipment

Mark this area if a vehicle component failed and contributed to the collision. Identify the defect and list the appropriate *vehicle code section if possible.*

Uninvolved Vehicle

This selection would be marked if one of the *involved parties* claims *another vehicle* contributed to the collision in some way. This element would be marked when the *other vehicle sustains no damage, and no evidence exists to establish the vehicle was involved.* This excludes *non-contact* vehicles that require a disinterested witness to verify the action(s) and vehicle code violation which caused the collision.

Other

This element would be marked when a factor *other than those listed above* is present such as a swerving maneuver to avoid an animal in the roadway, etc. The officer should explain the reason for this selection and any evidence which would support this conclusion.

Non-Apparent

This element is *self-explanatory* and should be marked when none of the elements explained above applies and no other associated factor exists.

Runaway Vehicle

This element should be checked when a vehicle is *accidentally set in motion* or *out of control* and which accelerates *uncontrollably* due to mechanical failure. This can include brake failure, stuck throttle, downshifting problems, or no steering. A person in the vehicle who is either unconscious or deceased while the vehicle is out of control would satisfy this requirement.

THE FINAL DECISION

Deciding on the appropriate *Primary Collision Factor* can present a challenge to even the most experienced traffic investigators. A given scenario may have several possible *P.C.F.'s* depending on the officers interpretation of the laws. Factors such as pursuit driving, D.U.I., and the lack of evidence at the scene may make it extremely difficult if not sometimes nearly impossible to determine. Seeking help and a second opinion on a complex investigation is advisable. A second opinion may prove very helpful when the collision is analyzed from an *outsider's view.*

THIS PAGE INTENTIONALLY LEFT BLANK

7

DRIVING UNDER THE INFLUENCE

INTRODUCTION

The National Highway Traffic Safety Administration estimates approximately *35%* of all fatal traffic collisions involve *alcohol* or *drugs*. Fifty percent of drivers killed have a blood alcohol level of *.10*. This was a 1990 statistic before the current blood alcohol level of *.08* took effect. Alcohol is readily available for consumption by the general public. Television and radio ads become a daily occurrence during the holiday season warning drivers of the penalties involving a D.U.I. arrest. The newspapers have printed numerous stories about the hazards of D.U.I, however this does not seem to stop those determined to *drive drunk*. We continue to read several news stories each year concerning D.U.I. related accidents or fatalities.

Alcohol and driving should never be mixed!

The California Highway Patrol reported that *84* suspected drunk drivers were arrested during the 78 hour enforcement period of the New Year's Eve weekend. In the past three years San Bernardino County has logged at least *one* traffic-related fatality on New Year's Eve or New Year's Day. In 1994, more than *97,000* California motorists were arrested for D.U.I. Most of those people who were arrested spent hundreds of dollars in fines and attorney's fees. Alcohol related accidents are much more deadly due to the lack of reaction time by the D.U.I. driver.

D.U.I. RELATED COLLISIONS

Chapter 6 discussed alcohol related traffic collisions and the part they play in making a determination of the *primary collision factor*. The D.U.I. accident however, presents an interesting twist to the *misdemeanor rule*. A California peace officer *must* witness the act to make a misdemeanor arrest. The traffic collision related D.U.I. contact is an *exception* to this hard and fast rule. *40300.5 CVC* provides authority for a peace officer to make a misdemeanor arrest for an incident that occurred out of his presence. The key factor in the language of this exception is the question: *"Does the officer have reasonable cause to believe the suspect was driving under the influence at the time of the collision?"* Once this has been established, you may arrest the suspect even though the driving did *not* occur in your presence. The following language can be found in section *40300.5 CVC.*

(A) The person was involved in a *"traffic accident"* (Jordan 1977) 75 Cal.App.3d Supp. 1, or

(B) The person is *"in or about"* a vehicle which is obstructing the roadway. (Ashley 1971) 17 Cal.App.3d 122

These above listed appellate court rulings' support the effort of the law enforcement professional trying to apprehend persons driving under the influence. The law may be interpreted liberally when investigating traffic related D.U.I. collisions. The collision must involve the vehicle being driven while D.U.I. and striking any other object. This may include a tree, person, other vehicle, or animal. For example the collision may involve the suspect's own vehicle with no other outside collateral damage.

Example:

A suspect driving under the influence leaves the roadway, goes over an embankment, and becomes *stuck* in the sand. A moped strikes a curb and the driver *falls over*. The word *accident* means *any* undesirable or unexpected event or mishap. Both of these examples were found to fall within the parameters of section *40300.5 CVC*, and their respective state appeals were denied.

D.U.I. CORPUS DELECTI RULE

We face a major obstacle in investigating D.U.I. related traffic collisions. Once the officer arrives, the driver is not always seated behind the wheel of the vehicle. He or she may be walking around the vehicle or standing outside among other passengers. Officers often contact the suspected driver and merely ask *"Where you driving the vehicle?"* If the suspect admits being the driver, we must also prove he/she were D.U.I. by other supporting circumstantial evidence. The California court system requires the *elements* of driving under influence be proven *independently* of the suspect's *own admission.* The question can then be posed, *"How can we prove the driver did it?"* This may be accomplished in several ways:

In People vs. Garcia *(1983) 149 Ca3d Sup 50* the defendant was involved in a traffic collision. The officer arrived and found four subjects standing by the damaged pick-up truck. The officer approached the subject closest to the truck and asked, *"Were you driving?"* The subject told the officer he was driving the truck. The officer did not stop here but continued his investigation by asking each additional passenger if they were driving the pick-up. Each passenger said they were not the driver and shrugged their shoulders when asked who was the driver if they weren't. This case was upheld because the officer used *"the process of elimination"* in his investigation.

In People Vs Nelson *(1985) 140 Ca3d Sup1* the officer responded to a rollover collision. He arrived and found each of the two occupants had been thrown from the vehicle during the collision. A witness said each of the two injured parties had been thrown from the vehicle, but could not point to the driver. The officer approached the injured party nearest to the vehicle and asked, *"Were you driving the vehicle?"* The subject admitted he was the driver and was arrested. The officer did not however, interview the 2nd party to confirm he was not the driver. The court overturned this case stating the officer did not use *"the process of elimination"* to establish the corpus of the crime. The driver's statements alone were not acceptable.

In People vs. Moreno *(1987) 188 Ca3d Sup 1179* the officer again only asked the suspected driver if he was driving the vehicle at the time of the collision. The court however issued some suggested guidelines for assisting the officer in proving corpus in this type of contact. The court stated the corpus may be proved by the following process:

- *Using the process of elimination.*
- *Interviewing bystanders who may point to the identity of the driver.*
- *Any physical evidence found at the scene e.g. prints, ID, car keys, etc.*

The officer is not precluded from making the inference based on the distance the suspected driver was found from the vehicle if a *nexus* exists. The suspect may be the registered owner of the vehicle that was located at the scene of the collision.

In People vs. Komatsu *(1989) 212 Ca3d Sup1* the officer located a vehicle obstructing the roadway at 2400 hours. The taillights of the vehicle were on, but the engine was not running. The officer made his approach and located a subject sleeping in the passenger's seat. The subject was found to have the keys to the vehicle in his pocket. The vehicle was not registered to him, however it was registered to a family member at the same address. The court stated the officer had used other present *circumstantial evidence* to prove the corpus of the crime including the suspect's own admission.

In People Vs Gapelu *(1989) 216 Ca3d Sup 1006* the officer arrived and found a person standing *near* the vehicle. This subject had glass imbedded in his elbow and was bleeding from the injury. He also had a cut on his forehead and glass in his hair. Gapelu admitted he was the driver, however the officer did not stop with only his admission. The officer looked into the vehicle and found the steering wheel was bent and the windshield was cracked where the driver would have been sitting. He noted the passengers seat had slammed forward impacting the dash. Gapelu's injuries were consistent with what he had found on the driver's side of the vehicle. Gapelu also did not have any leg injuries which would have been the case had he been sitting in the passengers seat. The officer supported the admission with several key pieces of circumstantial evidence in his investigation to establish the corpus of this crime.

The following will be list of possible recommendations when investigating a D.U.I. related traffic collision:

1. *Ask every person present if they were driving the vehicle. Also ask them who was driving the vehicle. This removes any possible defense that may be brought up later at a trial.*

2. *Observe and record the relative distance the suspect was located from the vehicle. Also note the distance of each of the remaining passengers to the vehicle.*

3. *Check the registration and confirm the owner's name. Look for a possible personalized plate or other moniker on the vehicle that might place the suspect in an ownership position.*

4. *Examine any keys that have been found on the suspect. Check each key with the ignition of the vehicle. Ask the suspect if he/she has knowledge of any of the other keys located on the vehicle's key ring.*

5. *Note whether the driver's seat is in the forward or rear position. Record the various heights of the suspects and passengers. Is the vehicle's seat in a position that is consistent with the height of the suspected driver?*

6. *Is the suspect familiar with the controls of the vehicle?*

7. *Consider impounding the vehicle in a fatal or serious injury traffic collision. Check for fingerprints on the driver's door and mirror and also fingerprint the passenger side of the vehicle. A sober passenger may claim he was the driver until his prints are placed on the passenger side of the vehicle.*

A D.U.I. related collision investigation can provide you with one of the rare opportunities to make a misdemeanor arrest without the driving being committed in your presence.

FIELD SOBRIETY TESTS

The smell of alcohol on the driver's breath and person should make you suspicious of a driver being under the influence of alcohol. Accident related D.U.I. investigations may be difficult due to the possible injuries the driver receives in the incident itself. For this reason, the objective symptoms of D.U.I. become very important. Drivers with injuries may not be able to perform the standard field sobriety test. Your decision regarding the driver's impairment will be almost completely based on the objective symptoms alone. Make the life saving effort in your collision scene management your first and utmost priority. Once this has been accomplished, look for any objective symptoms of intoxication. The fire personnel may be the first to alert you of this possibility. They will be working closely with the injured drivers and may smell the alcohol long before you have a chance to interview the victim.

If the driver is severely injured, be sure to note the objective symptoms you have observed. Based on these observations, you may be able to justify making an arrest for the offense of driving under the influence. The driver may need transportation to a nearby hospital for treatment; and therefore, field sobriety tests may not be performed.

The driver who is walking and appears not to be injured will be handled in the same manner as a suspected D.U.I. stop on the highway. The D.U.I. driver will cause you to reorganize some of the activities performed at the collision scene. You may wish to detail an officer to assist you with the D.U.I. portion of the accident investigation. This will allow you to keep your attention primarily directed toward collision scene management. The assigned officer will handle the field sobriety tests, D.U.I. processing, and all needed paperwork to add to the collision report.

Keep your field sobriety test simple but to the point. Each officer has a set of tests with which he or she is comfortable. Have the driver walk away from the activity at the main collision scene. The rotating lights, radio equipment, and police personnel may be distracting to the person attempting to concentrate on the tests you request he/she perform. Start the testing by asking many of the questions that are found on your F.S.T. forms. Questions such as alcohol consumption, pre-existing disabilities and medications can all be asked without the required Miranda advisement.

One of the most important questions in this type of D.U.I. contact will be *"Have you been drinking since the collision?"* A driver may later claim, in court, that he or she consumed 3-4 additional beers while waiting for you to arrive at the scene. This may not seem important, but officers have lost cases in court under similar circumstances. This becomes a more significant issue in a D.U.I. related hit and run. These questions may derail a defense of this type at a later date. A suspected driver will not be able to prove his blood alcohol rose as a result of the alcohol he consumed after he fled from the collision scene. Suspects have offered the defense they drank additional alcohol due to being scared and nervous after they fled from the scene.

D.U.I. RELATED EVIDENCE

Each officer reading this book should have already received training in the handling of D.U.I. related physical evidence, or will in the near future. So here are just some basics. There are three ways to test for a person's blood alcohol level. *Blood* testing is the most popular and produces the most accurate measurement. *Breath* is the second most popular form of measuring a person's level of intoxication. The breath test gives the officer an instantaneous readout. The *Urine* test is becoming less and less used due to the suspect's inability to complete the test. The suspect must provide a sample of his or her urine, then void the remainder of his/her bladder. The implied consent law is valid, and the driver may choose the test he/she wishes to take. Be sure to check your state's current laws and your departmental policy in regards to using these tests.

Each department has guidelines for obtaining evidence in felony cases. Many departments allow the officer to *force* a blood test if necessary depending on the severity of the crime or collision. The best way to approach this situation may be to simply *ask* his/her permission in a respectful manner. Advise the suspect a blood test will be taken, and his/her cooperation is requested. Force should always be a *last resort.* Tell the suspect you will note his refusal in the report if this makes him comply with your request. The suspect will usually physically resist you until the needle is near the arm. The court looks at forced blood tests in a reasonable fashion. They have stated in part the need to obtain evidence must be balanced with the defendant's own safety. Therefore the procedure should not *"violate or shock the conscience of the court."*

The driver who is injured must be addressed quickly. He/she will be transported to the hospital and treated by emergency room personnel. The suspect may receive medication, "IV" solutions, and even additional blood when needed. All of these will have an effect on the evidence you wish to obtain. Depending on the case, you may decide to detail an officer to the hospital immediately to obtain a sample of the suspect's blood. Once you arrive, contact the emergency room nurse and ask if the sample may be obtained without interrupting any life-saving efforts already in progress.

Depending on your timing, the hospital nurse may have a full blood screen already ordered. The hospital blood technician will add your vial to the ones he/she will be taking. The suspect may be injured, but you have found the injuries are not life threatening. Make contact with the driver at the hospital and advise him you are still investigating the collision. Ask the preliminary questions discussed in the previous pages in reference to his or her alcohol consumption. The driver may be willing to comply with your request for a blood sample. If the driver is hostile, advise him/her that he/she is *under arrest.* This will give you the needed authority to obtain a blood sample without his consent. Once the sample is obtained, advise the suspect he is *being released*, and so note this in your report. Indicate the drivers injuries precluded you from booking the suspect for the violation.

D.U.I. REPORTS

A alcohol related traffic collision and arrest must be handled as *two* reports. Section *40300.5 CVC* provides an exception to the misdemeanor rule when making an arrest as a result of a traffic collision. For this reason, the accident report is necessary to support your probable cause in making the D.U.I. arrest. The accident report must be completed on a C.H.P. 555 with an accompanying narrative concluding the collision was the result of a D.U.I. The influence report does not need to duplicate what was said in the collision report. The D.U.I. narrative should describe your contact with the suspected driver and your supporting conclusion of how he was identified as the driver. Be sure to use suggestions found in the earlier pages of this chapter.

D.U.I. AS A PRIMARY COLLISION FACTOR

In the previous chapters, we talked briefly about D.U.I. as a Primary Collision Factor or *P.C.F.* A driver who is found to be under the influence at the time of the investigation may also be listed as the P.C.F. in the collision. This would be limited to the collisions where the D.U.I. driver committed the act that was found to be the proximate cause of the accident. The act, or vehicle code violation, that caused the collision would be listed as the *associated factor*, with the D.U.I. or 23152(a) CVC becoming the P.C.F. Occasionally, the D.U.I. driver did not cause the collision, but was simply in the wrong place at the wrong time. The cause of the accident would become the listed vehicle code violation for party #1. The D.U.I. or 23152(A) CVC would be listed as an *associated factor* for the party who was found to be under the influence, but not at fault in the accident.

ADDITIONAL HELP

There is a great deal of resource material on this subject. LawTech publishes several different sources of information relating to D.U.I. enforcement such as *The Street Cop's Guide to Drunk Driving Enforcement* and *Peace Officers' Legal Source Guide - California Edition*, which contains information relating to the legalities of making D.U.I. arrests. The State of California also publishes a book entitled *California Peace Officers' Legal Source Book*, which has an entire chapter dedicated to the legalities of making D.U.I. arrests. I would also recommend you take a class at your local police or sheriff's academy specifically on this subject. The laws change frequently, however, the general public and California courts are supportive of your actions in this area of traffic collision investigation. Many groups such as M.A.D.D. (Mothers Against Drunk Drivers) are constantly applying pressure to the legislative branch of our judicial system. Keeping current in this area of traffic enforcement will give you a distinct advantage when encountering a D.U.I. related traffic collision.

8

COLLISION INVESTIGATION PROCEDURES

INTRODUCTION

Once the dust begins to settle at a collision scene, the true investigative work begins. The traffic officer must move quickly to gather all of the needed information to complete his or her investigation. After the scene has been cleared, it becomes difficult to track down driver information and potential witness statements. You must balance the need for opening the street with gathering important evidence. Many officers have been rushed in the investigation stage resulting in missed information or physical evidence. A balance must be found between these two important issues. We will discuss many of the investigative cues that will assist you in justifying further in-depth investigation.

Physical evidence comes in many forms. Traffic collision related evidence must be classified based on its importance to the investigator. Roadway gouge marks, skidmarks, and vehicle debris are but just a few of these pieces of evidence. Sometimes the vehicles themselves can provide the accident investigator with important clues as to how the collision took place. Evidence at a collision scene will either support or refute a statement received from a witness or driver. We will examine some of the more important pieces of evidence commonly found at an accident scene.

COMPARING NOTES

Once the collision scene becomes manageable, compare the information you have received from the first responding officer with what you have observed by walking the scene. Does the scenario presented to you match the physical evidence at the scene? Do the independent witness statements support your early conclusions? These are but just a few of the questions you should be asking yourself while still evaluating the scene. Step back away from the confusion of all of the emergency personnel and reevaluate all of the information you have received. If any of these questions appear not to have been answered to your satisfaction, clarify the information before it becomes too late. If you are the primary handling officer, you must decide who will be responsible for each of the basic parts of the collision investigation. A secondary officer at the scene can assist you by gathering vehicle information. You may choose to handle *all* of the interviews making the investigation less complicated.

INTERVIEWING TECHNIQUES FOR YOUR WITNESSES

Make contact with independent witnesses as early in the investigation as possible. Witnesses have a tendency to remain at the scene due to the severity of the impact. Gaining a quick brief statement or a phone number from a witness for a later interview may support your decision of what caused the collision. A disinterested witness may have either a very simplified or a very complicated statement to provide you. Your job is to distract them from the overall visual and psychological impact of the scene. You will then try to view the collision through their eyes. Third parties may explain the accident as if you should know *exactly* what they are talking about. At times, you must have an extraordinary amount of patience in dealing with witnesses about vehicle direction and speeds. Witnesses have been known to place the vehicles in totally opposite directions than the evidence supports. They also may either over estimate or under estimate the speeds of the vehicles involved.

Interviewing a witness properly at a traffic collision scene is very important. The decisions you make at the conclusion of your investigation may hinge directly on the statements provided to you by a disinterested witness. For this reason alone, obtaining a thorough interview becomes that much more important. Witnesses have a tendency to *"rattle on"* when talking about traffic collisions. A direct approach of asking questions may expedite this process. The following will be list of possible suggested questions you may wish to ask in addition to the questions posed about the collision.

- *"Can you show me where you were standing when you observed the collision?"*
- *"Were you driving a car or walking on foot at the time you saw the collision?"*
- *"Can you point out to me who was driving which vehicle?"*
- *"How fast was each of the vehicles traveling just before they collided?"*
- *"Do you know any of the parties involved in the collision?"*

Some of the above questions may clarify what a witness could have seen from his/her respective vantage point. These answers can become extremely important in the more complex collision investigations. A sharp attorney may be able to discredit your star witness years after the collision with these same questions. It is doubtful that your memory is good enough to recall what a witness told you two or three years after the collision. After completing your interview, quickly review and read back the statement to the witness. This assures the information was received properly.

DRIVERS' STATEMENTS

A driver's statement may sometimes be difficult to gain depending on the severity of the injuries received in the impact. The majority of the accidents you will investigate may be a moderate injury type collision. These interviews will present somewhat of a challenge to accomplish at the scene. Timing may play a key factor in talking with a injured driver. Once the drivers are removed from their respective vehicles the rescue personnel have a small amount of *lag* time before they transport their patients to area hospitals. This might become just the right opportunity for you to talk briefly with the drivers. Contact the paramedics and ask them if you may quickly talk with the injured parties and passengers.

Depending on the injuries and the psychological impact of the collision, the involved parties may or may not remember what happened in the accident. This is not uncommon and should not hopefully become a source of frustration for you. Traumatic incidents may blank out the memory of the drivers for a period of time. Depending on the impact, some parties never regain a full memory of the events during the collision. The decision to follow-up the interview at the hospital rests with you. The information you are seeking might be better gained from a less severely injured passenger.

A driver's statement is considered *biased* simply because of his/her interest in becoming exonerated in the incident. Often times even while facing overwhelming physical evidence and witness statements, the driver at fault will not admit his or her mistake. Remember to verify which vehicle each driver was in before the fire department arrived. This sounds basic, but reports have been submitted for review which have these parties reversed. Your credibility in court at a later date may depend on the professional appearance of your investigation. The following is a checklist of suggested items to use while interviewing a driver in a traffic collision.

- Does the driver match the photo and description of his or her license?
- Does the driver have an *odor of alcohol* on his/her breath and person during your contact?
- Is the driver restricted to wearing *corrective lenses* while driving and was he or she wearing them at the time of the impact?
- Is the driver of either vehicle an *intravenous drug user*? Note which symptoms are present to substantiate this speculation. Note what type of injuries the driver has received from the collision, and if he has been *medicated by the rescue personnel*?
- The above list helps me to understand the credibility of the driver's statement. A driver who is severely injured and who has received pain medication may distort the facts. For this reason, a later interview may be appropriate. One the other hand, a intoxicated driver may provide you with information while under the influence which will support prosecution for the offense. If one of the drivers is to be charged with a crime of manslaughter, remember to *Mirandize* him/her if you intend to make an arrest for the crime. However, if the injuries to the suspected driver are such that he or she will not be arrested, then Miranda does not apply. The true test of Miranda is

whether the party is *detained* and is *not free to leave*. Several publications including *The Peace Officers Legal Resource Book published, by the State of California, or the Field Legal SourceGuide, published by LawTech,* are available for reference material on this subject.

PASSENGER STATEMENTS

Passengers in the involved vehicles are not considered independent witnesses due to their potential relationship with the driver. The separation process during the interview stage may be enough to isolate a prepared witness. Passengers will discuss the collision out loud in front of many people before you arrive. This may prejudice other passengers who are willing to talk with you about what *really* may have taken place. Ask the passengers where they were seated in the vehicle and what they observed from their vantage point. Ask if they were talking with the driver or any of the other passengers just before the collision? Passengers will at times paint themselves into a corner about what was taking place just before the accident. This either will discredit them from claiming the driver did anything wrong, or support the driver's claim in the collision.

INJURIES

Ask each of the parties involved if they have been injured as a result of the accident. This technique will help to preclude he/she from coming into the station after the fact to complain they were injured in the collision. As stated earlier, ads for attorneys have saturated the television airwaves. Parties who were not injured at the scene suddenly become injured once they have talked with an attorney. No one expects you to be a doctor in your evaluation, but simply ask, *"Where does it hurt?"* Each party injured in the accident must be listed on the *"Injury/Witness"* page of the C.H.P. 555.

AREA OF IMPACT

The definition of Area of Impact is the location, point or area where a vehicle comes into contact with another vehicle, object, or surface as a result of a traffic collision. The *P.O.I.* or *point of impact* is often referred to as the *area of impact* or *A.O.I.* A collision may contain many *A.O.I.'s* depending on the number of vehicles involved and the number of objects or surfaces with which the vehicle comes into contact in the process.

The A.O.I. may be determined by vehicle debris, skidmark distortion, or gouging in the roadway. Occasionally these above clues do not exist and a rough guess is necessary. A witness, driver, or passenger may be able to point to the area where the collision took place. Thus the name *area of impact* rather than *point of impact* is more widely used. This also alleviates a possible argument by an attorney who likes to *"split hairs"* when discussing this area of your *collision investigation report.*

Often times multiple areas of impact may exist. A three car collision may have three or more A.O.I.'s. Check the ground carefully for those above listed clues to determine where the collision first took place. The A.O.I. may be hidden under a piece of emergency rescue equipment. If a skidmark exists, begin walking toward the accident scene from the beginning of the skid. Look for a distortion in the somewhat straight pattern of the skid. This would indicate an outside force acted on the vehicle's movement causing the angular change in the mark.

Standing back away from the scene will allow you to view the entire scene.
You may then possibly observe additional Areas of Impact.

Examine the roadway for a possible gouge mark that might have been left by a vehicle digging into the surface. These marks may have been the first point of contact with either another vehicle or a fixed object. Other supporting evidence around the gouge mark such as vehicle debris or a skidmark distortion may aide in your possible conclusion.

Use caution in your roadway and A.O.I. analysis. Remember many other vehicle collisions may have occurred in the same intersection and therefore evidence may still be present to confuse you in your investigation. Skidmarks from a previous incident may look as if they are involved in the current accident. We will discuss basic skidmark analysis in Chapter 10.

A.O.I. MEASUREMENTS

The area of impact must be measured and documented in your *collision investigation.* This may be accomplished in many ways. The face sheet of your collision investigation report requires you to list the *primary street* where the accident took place. A second measurement in feet or tenths of a mile will be necessary to properly document where the collision occurred. For example, the collision may have taken place on *Sierra Ave.* s/of *Merrill Ave.* The face sheet of your report requires you to estimate of how far s/of the intersection the accident occurred.

This required measurement can be taken in several different ways. The most accurate measuring device would be a *steel or fiberglass tape*, however not all police units are equipped with this tool. This type of tape will give a consistent measurement without movement and will remain in place throughout the investigation process.

Steel or fiberglass tapes, similar to the one pictured above on the center lane line, are the most accurate means of obtaining a collision scene measurement.

The second most desirable tool would be a *roll-a-tape*. This type of measuring tool is more commonly found in patrol units. This device has an extended handle, wheels for walking the tool in any direction, and somewhat easy to read numbers. The third and most in-accurate way of measuring would be by *pacing*. Pacing may vary depending on the natural stride of the investigating officer. Whatever measuring tool you decide upon, try to be as consistent as possible.

The area of impact has been determined, but how is it measured for the accident report? Two measurements to a single point are necessary for documentation in a diagram or report. The majority of intersections are shaped in the form of a box or rectangle. For this reason the accident scene and intersection may be split into *four parts* as follows:

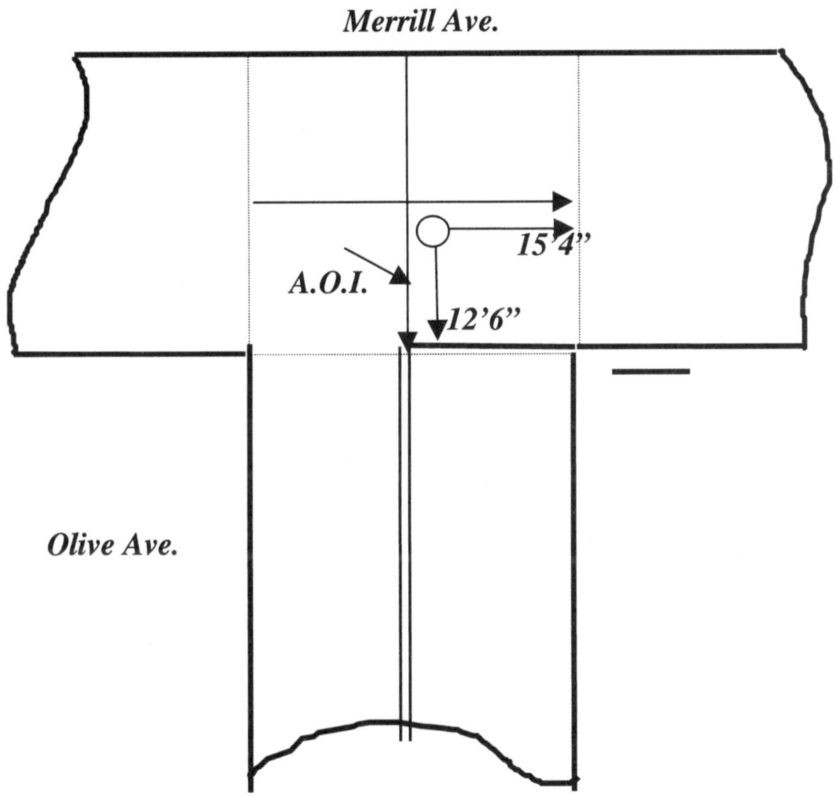

In the example above, the collision was restricted to an intersection. We can measure the A.O.I. to two different points within the intersection itself. The face sheet of this report would read as follows. The collision occurred on *Merrill Ave.* at *Olive Ave.* The area of impact however must be measured from two locations at the collision scene. The measurements may be taken from a *curb line*, a *prolongation of a curb line*, or a *roadway edge*. Each A.O.I. must be evaluated for a measurement that will be the easiest to gather based on the terrain of the scene.

Once the A.O.I. has been located, try to take the measurements to the nearest curb. In the example above, the intersection has been divided into *four major quadrants*. This quadrant system helps us to visualize the nearest two curbs or curb line prolongations. After identifying these locations, we may take our measurements and document the area of impact for the collision investigation. You are by no means restricted to measuring to the nearest two curbs and may measure to the curbs on the opposite side of the roadway.

The measurement taken on the previous page should be taken using a roll-a-tape or steel tape if at all possible. Pacing is acceptable but has the most room for error. After taking the measurements, we may either place them in *one of two* places in the report. A heading of *Area of Impact* may be added to your investigative narrative, or you may use the *miscellaneous* box of the C.H.P. 555 (adjacent to the sketch area of the report). The A.O.I. on the previous page would be written as follows:

A.O.I. The A.O.I. was found to be approximately *15'4"* w/of the *e/c/l/p* of *Olive Ave.* & approximately *12'6"* n/of the *s/c/l/p* of *Merrill Ave.* The measurements were taken with a roll-a-tape.

The above description of the *area of impact* is simplified by using acronyms for some of the longer references, *e.g. s/c/l/p and e/c/l/p.* The longer references to *South curb line prolongation & East curb line prolongation* may be written in their entirety if it makes the definition easier to remember.

Look for the deviation or change in a straight skidmark that will assist you in locating the A.O.I.

If the collision occurs outside of the intersection, the roadway may be divided in half by the natural lane markings. A measurement should be taken to the nearest roadway edge or curb. The secondary measurement can be taken to the nearest curb line prolongation. In the following example, Merrill Ave. is the closest intersection to the A.O.I. We can therefore utilize this intersection prolongation line to determine and mark our second measurement. The face sheet of the report would read: *"The collision occurred on Olive Ave."* (check the box directly below marked "or") and list how many feet s/of the intersection the accident took place. The A.O.I. of this collision was found to measure approximately *24'8"* s/of *Merrill Ave.* Listing the curb line prolongation *is not* necessary on the face sheet of the report.

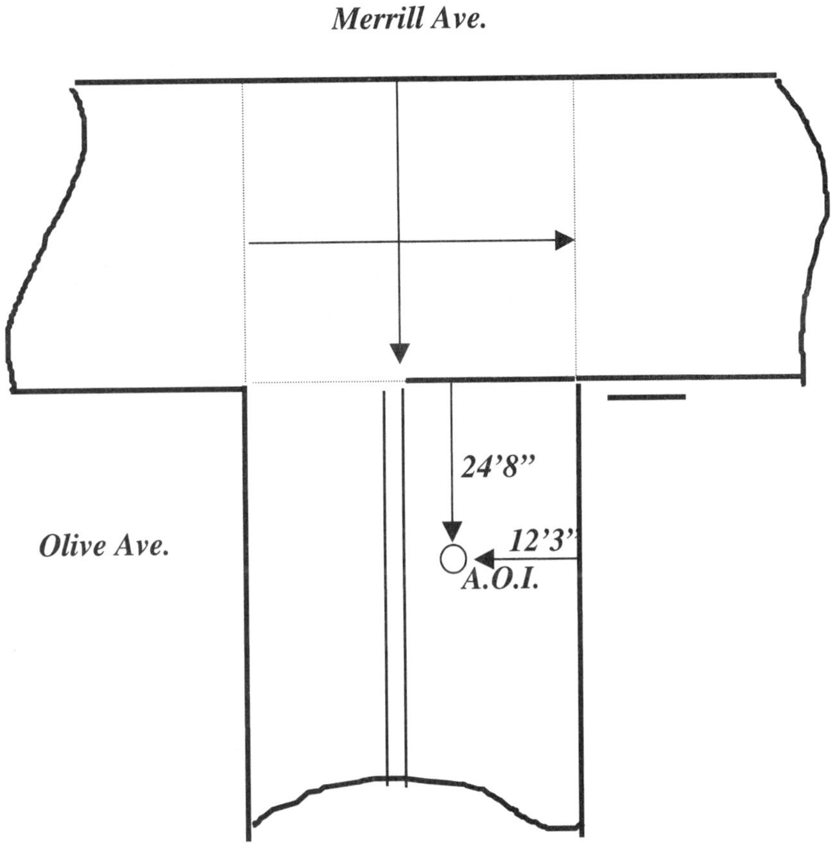

A.O.I. The A.O.I. was found to be approximately *12'3"* w/of the *e/c/l* (east curb line) of *Olive Ave.* & approximately *24'8"* s/of the *s/c/l/p* (south curb line prolongation) of *Merrill Ave.* The measurements were taken with a roll-a-tape.

Traffic collisions may also be measured or estimated using your police vehicle. Many times a collision takes place miles away from the nearest intersection. For this reason, an estimate using your police vehicle is acceptable. The face sheet of the accident report allows the investigator to measure in *miles* or *feet*. The first measurement to the roadway edge should still be obtained using the system demonstrated in the previous examples. The second measurement however may be calculated using your police vehicles *"trip meter." "Zero out"* the tenths counter at the A.O.I. and drive to the nearest *cross street* or *mile marker*. For those not familiar with *"mile markers"*, they can best be described as a metal marker approximately 3-4 feet in height and often found along side of the road or highway in more rural areas. The marker is white in color and has a number painted on it near the top.

This collision could be measured either with tapes or using a vehicle's odometer as shown in the example below.

Collision Occurred On **Lytle Creek Ave.**
☐ ■ 2/10 ~~Feet~~*Miles* **South** *of* **Duncan Canyon Rd**

The collision pictured above would be written on the C.H.P. 555 as demonstrated above. Remember the main difference in the two is the A.O.I. requires *two* measurements whereas the face sheet listing requires the *main street* and *one other* measurement only. Measuring the A.O.I. is not meant to be a tricky task. Take your time and pick the points that appear to be the easiest for you to document. The same principles may be used when investigating a collision that occurs on *private property*. Measurements should be taken toward the *two nearest streets* using the same documentation method as described on the previous pages. Off-road areas will require a calculated estimate by driving or walking to the nearest known roadway.

EVIDENCE INTERPRETATION

One of the more interesting issues in accident investigation is that, unlike a homicide, the majority of evidence remains at the scene. The largest and most significant piece of evidence is the *suspect vehicle*. The suspect vehicle itself can tell a trained investigator many things about the collision. Knowing what to look for in a vehicle inspection is not difficult. This can at times be overlooked in the totality of the circumstances. The severity of the traffic collision will dictate the need for a thorough vehicle inspection. You will ultimately make the decision on this issue while still at the scene. Conclusions of how the accident occurred can be reinforced by evidence located in a vehicle while still at the scene.

Look closely; the front license plate contains a month and year tab. Could this plate belong to another vehicle? What other things could be wrong with this vehicle?

By no means are you to expected to become a mechanic in order to understand the inner workings of a vehicle. A basic understanding of how a vehicle works is all that is needed.

The accident investigator is looking for *obvious* signs of stress in the vehicle. This may include inspecting the lower frame of the vehicle for any cracks or distortion that would provide you with a *principal direction of force*. The interior of the vehicle can also provide many clues about the accident. The position of the *turn signal* or *gear shift* may support a statement gained from one of the drivers as to his/her preparation to make a turning movement.

The following check list of items that should be inspected visually each time you investigate a collision, particularly fatals and those involving major injuries.

Vehicle Inspection Checklist

Braking System: If skidmarks are present, the vehicles braking system is working. What condition is the *master cylinder* in? The fluid in the system might have been extremely low and may have contributed to the collision. Are the *disk brake pads* visible to you and what is the wear level?

Tires: What are the sizes and inflation levels of the tires? Are the tires made to safely operate on this size rim? What is the current tread depth on the tires?

Wheel Lugs: Count and inspect the wheel lugs on each tire/rim set.

Vehicle Lighting: Were the lights on and activated at the time of the collision? Check the lighting indicator or switch inside of the vehicle. A witness may also validate this issue if the indicator has been damaged.

Interior Check: Check the interior for any signs of open containers that may support your suspicions of the accident being alcohol related.

Windshield: Check the windshield for damage that would be consistent with the injuries sustained by the driver or passenger. Also look for any cracking or obstructions which may have been present before the collision.

Injuries: Note the injuries received by each of the occupants in the vehicle. Due to the collision, these parties may honestly not remember where they were seated in the vehicle.

Seatbelts: What is the condition of the seatbelts in the vehicle? Newer vehicles have seatbelts that automatically retract into the door post. Did the rescue personnel cut the seatbelts? Are the seatbelts tucked into positions under the seats, unable to be worn?

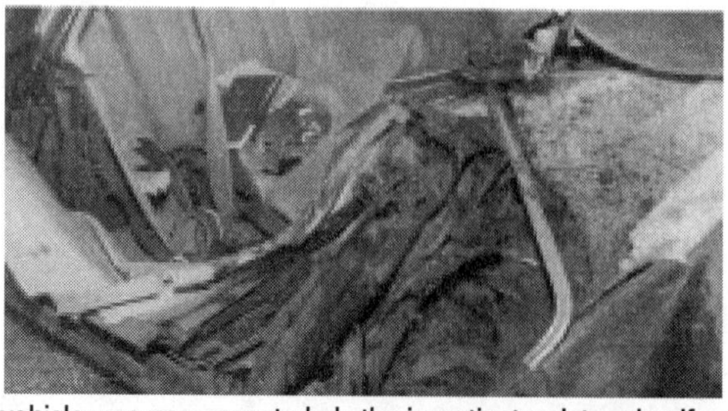

A close inspection of this vehicle was necessary to help the investigator determine if seatbelts were in fact worn.

Speedometer: Check the speedometer and look for *"Slapping"* on the face of the unit. Slapping has occurred in high speed collisions when a large amount of stopping force is involved. A mark is sometimes left upon the face of the unit that will be visible.

Gear Shift: In what gear was the vehicle found at the time of your inspection? This is a more valid concern on a manual transmission. Often the driver will say he or she was traveling at a very slow speed and could not have been going as fast as suspected. The vehicle may have been in *fourth* gear at the time and would validate a witness' statement.

Turn Signals: If the lighting system and battery have been disconnected in the collision, you will not be able to check the lighting system. This is a concern in an *"unsafe speed"* collision where the striking driver claimed the other vehicle did not signal while waiting to turn into a driveway.

Tire Position: What direction or position are the vehicle's tires in at the time of the inspection? This can assist you in substantiating a statement by a driver he or she was waiting to make a turn.

HOT & COLD SHOCK DEFORMATION

Many times the cause of the collision hinges on one or two very important issues. These can range from the vehicle's speed to the driver's alcohol or drug influence. Other times a claim is made by a witness, or other driver, stating one of the vehicles did not have its lights on at the time of the collision. Many of these questions can be answered with a thorough analysis. Unfortunately a vehicle's lighting system can be severely damaged in the collision making it all but impossible to check. The switch may have been broken, or the vehicle may be damaged beyond repair. Relying on a single witness is acceptable, however a technique has been developed to inspect a lamp filament. This will solve the mystery of whether the lights were on or off at the time of impact independent of the much sought-after witness statement.

To accomplish this technique one must understand what we call the *Principal direction of force*. Principal direction of force is best described as the direction the vehicle's parts or cargo (passengers) will travel when impacted. A vehicle that impacts a stationary vehicle will suddenly apply a great deal of force in the direction it was moving. This force impacts the stationary vehicle with several follow-up impacts. The naked eye cannot observe these many additional collisions. For this reason, the fender that strikes the stationary vehicle is slowing down as the rear of the same vehicle is still traveling at the original speed. The stationary vehicle is then absorbing a majority of the impact by the vehicle striking it.

Many of you may have seen these slow motion accidents viewed from the inside of a vehicle. The Department of Transportation demonstrates the impact in a collision as seen from the interior of the vehicle. The plastic *"dummy"* continues into the windshield as the vehicle itself is coming to rest after striking an object. This occurs because the passengers in the vehicle are not rigidly affixed to the interior and are considered *flexible.* The flexible objects (passengers) will move in whatever direction from which the force is received. The filament in a bulb functions in a similar manner. The filament is flexible and can bend. For this reason it follows the same pattern.

The flexibility in a filament is gained from the heat generated when the bulb is hot. The heat produced illuminates the filament. This heat also makes the filament susceptible to damage or sudden impact. Non-illuminated filaments are brittle due to the filament being *cold.* This is an important distinction when inspecting a filament in a traffic collision.

The easiest way to inspect a bulb would be to remove it from the chassis at the scene of the collision. The general rule is to remove the bulb from the area closest to the portion of the vehicle where the impact was greatest. For example, at night you may also wish to check the rear tail lamp assembly for illumination if the front of the vehicle was destroyed in the accident. Use a screwdriver or pry tool and carefully remove the plastic cover from the assembly. This will expose the bulb for inspection. Remove the entire assembly rather than only the bulb. This will alleviate any questions at the time of trial that the bulb was removed from another vehicle rather than the one involved in the incident. Photograph the process that will serve as documentation the removal was done at the scene. Take one photo at each step showing the progress of removing the bulb and assembly. Many defense attorneys will attempt to argue the bulb was damaged at the time it was removed.

Cold Fracture

The tungsten filament is very brittle when the bulb is not activated and *cold*. The filament may break anywhere on the coil upon a sudden shock as in a traffic collision. The filament may also still be attached to the main arch of the bulb and remain unaffected by the impact. The cold fracture is a sign the bulb was *off* at the time of impact. The coil will appear still somewhat tightly wound as in the photo below.

The lamp above was off at the time of impact. The coil is still intact.

HOT SHOCK DEFORMATION

The lamp pictured below was *on* at the time of impact. The coiled filament is stretched but still attached at the time of our inspection. Incandescence or heat generated from the filament made the coil flexible. The sudden forward impact stretched this filament but did not break it. This bulb was removed from the tail lamp assembly of a vehicle involved in a head-on collision. The stretching is evident from the impact itself, however the filament was hot at the time of the impact and did not break.

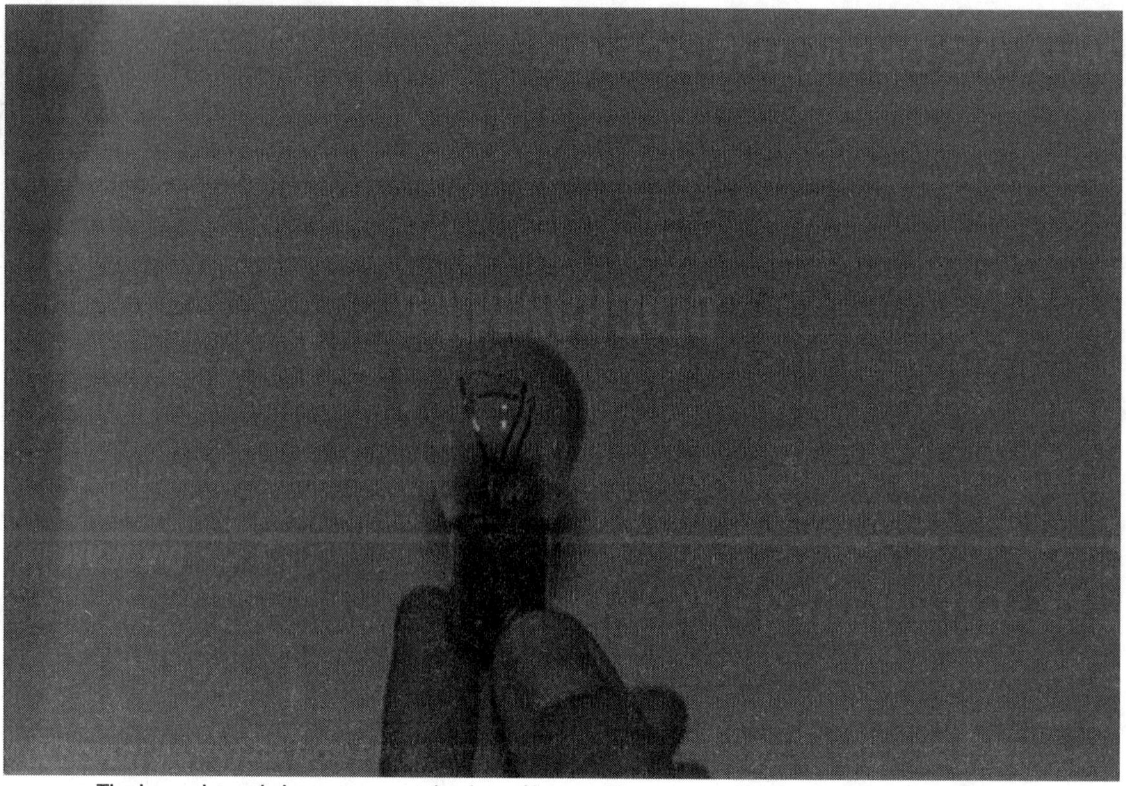

The lamp pictured above was on at the time of impact. The tungsten filament is somewhat distorted.

9

DIAGRAMMING

WHY WE DRAW THE SCENE?

The best way to view an entire traffic collision scene is from above. This however is not always practical unless the conditions are just right. The scene can be reproduced using careful documentation techniques allowing a view from above after the scene has been reproduced to scale on paper. Accident investigators do not need a degree in drafting or engineering. Collision scene diagramming is not complicated, particularly with the many diagramming aids available on the market today.

Once the scene has been measured and drawn to scale, collision analysis becomes more simplified. A quick reference to the attached diagram page of your report will yield the same information as the scene itself. Each significant piece of evidence will be reproduced on this drawing. The entire traffic collision scene may be viewed *at one time* and will become a quick reference guide for you when verifying your conclusions in later review.

SKETCH OR DIAGRAM?

Many of the collisions you investigate may not require a detailed *factual diagram*, and therefore an area on the C.H.P. 555 exists for a *sketch*. The sketch reflects the officer's *opinion* of how the accident occurred. Factual diagrams were required on each and every injury traffic collision investigated by many departments in the early 1980's. However, accident investigation has somewhat evolved since then, with the increase of reportable events. The reporting requirements have changed, giving more discretionary power to the investigating officer. The California Highway Patrol however, still completes a factual diagram on each and every *Investigation* type collision. Police agencies have begun to scale down their respective response to these collisions. The C.I.M. states the factual diagram *should* be completed for investigation collisions, but does not make it a mandatory requirement of the report. For this reason, many California agencies now complete a *sketch* only on an injury accident.

The sketch is specifically addressed in the C.I.M. in section *4*. The sketch is different from the factual diagram in that it shows *movement*. The sketch is not a snapshot of the aftermath but your opinion of the actions both preceding the collision, and to each of the successive A.I.O's. The C.I.M. describes each of the (4) symbols which may be used in the sketch. After reviewing these symbols, you will agree they represent *movement* and not an overview of the collision as in a factual diagram.

1. *Vehicle* (not parked) or a *bicycle*
2. *Pedestrian* or *animal*
3. *Train*
4. *Parked Vehicle*

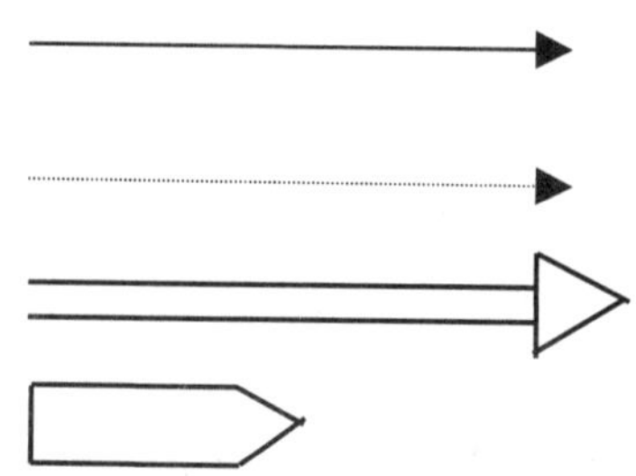

When completing a sketch, the majority of all collisions fall into *10* categories. The following will be examples of those above accident sketches. These examples may be rotated and placed into the drawn intersections of your respective cities.

1. *Head-on*
2. *Head-on sideswipe*
3. *Rear End*
4. *Overtaking sideswipe*
5. *Broadside*
6. *Approach turn*
7. *Overtaking turn*
8. *Out of control*
9. *Overturned (2 loops maximum)*
10. *Vehicle backing*

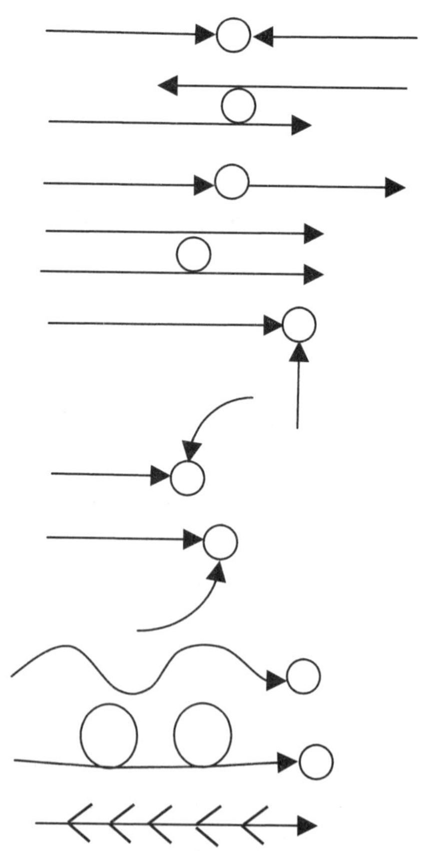

A sketch is required in each of the reports that will be investigated by your respective agencies. A sketch may be drawn *free hand* or by utilizing a template. A small straight edged object such as a credit card or ruler will suffice for this purpose. The sketch is one of the first areas an accident investigator will review and should *tell the story* of how the collision most likely took place. The sketch should be accurate and *does not* need to be a scaled diagram.

Include the street curbs, any relevant signs, and street names on the sketch. Trees, vehicle skidmarks, and vehicle debris is not necessary in a sketch. Remember the sketch is the officer's opinion of the movement *preceding the collision.* For this reason the arrows represent the movement of each of the vehicle unless of course the vehicle is parked.

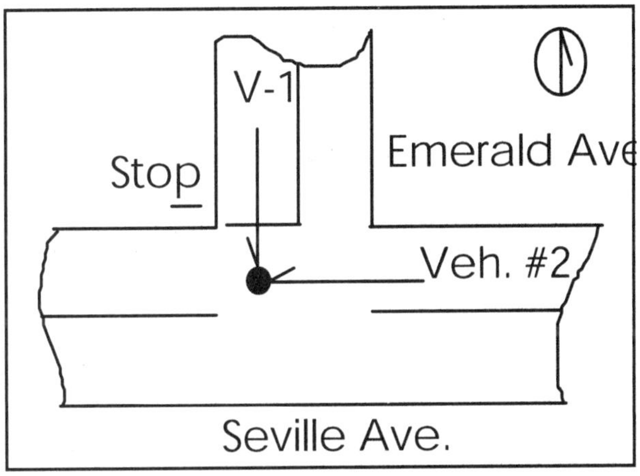

The above sketch represents a *broadside* collision occurring at a *"T"* style intersection. Vehicle #2 is approaching the intersection from the east traveling westbound. Vehicle number #1 is approaching the intersection from the north traveling southbound. By examining this sketch more closely, one can see a *stop sign* is posted on the northwest corner of the intersection for southbound traffic. Vehicle number #2 clearly has the right-of-way. Vehicle #1 has failed to stop for the posted stop sign and collided with vehicle #2.

As stated in the sketch examples, the arrows may be placed on sketches of intersections in your city. Make a sketch of the intersection then place the appropriate arrows on the diagram. The collision scene should be in proper proportion to the size of the streets. Be careful not to make a street wider or narrower than it exists in actuality. The streets should be identified along with a consistent direction for *North.* A common rule to follow is *North* should always point to the top of your sketch. Depending on the size of your sketch, you may wish to include a cross street for easier reference. All pertinent traffic control *stop signs or yield signs* along with crosswalks and limit lines should be included in your finished product. Include rocks, walls, and other objects that may have been impact locations in the collision.

Private property sketches should be drawn to the best of the officer's ability using the major streets which are nearest to the area of impact. Draw a structure in the sketch, if possible, to identify the location for easier reference. Label the structure by name and address, whenever practical. Parking spaces, driveways, and parked vehicles will all be left to the discretion of the investigating officer.

Remember the sketch is not a factual diagram, however the sketch should be drawn as neatly as possible. The sketch does not need to be drawn to scale, but a clear concise sketch will be one of the first items a reviewing officer will look for. A hand drawn sketch without the aide of a straight edge will look sloppy and unprofessional. Pen is acceptable but not recommended simply for the problem of correcting a mistake. Take your time to reproduce an accurate product of what took place.

The following will be a series of sketches depicting the most common types of accidents listing the P.C.F. directly below the diagram for easy reference.

Primary Collision Factor Sketches

Rear end collisions

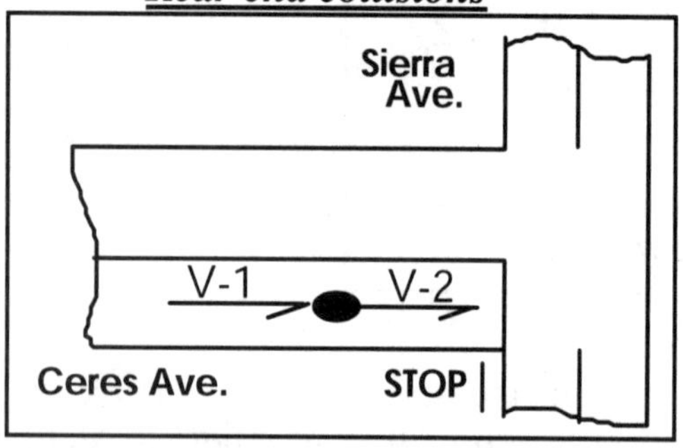

CVC 22350 Unsafe speed if V-2 is stopped when rear ended.

Right or left turns from a stop

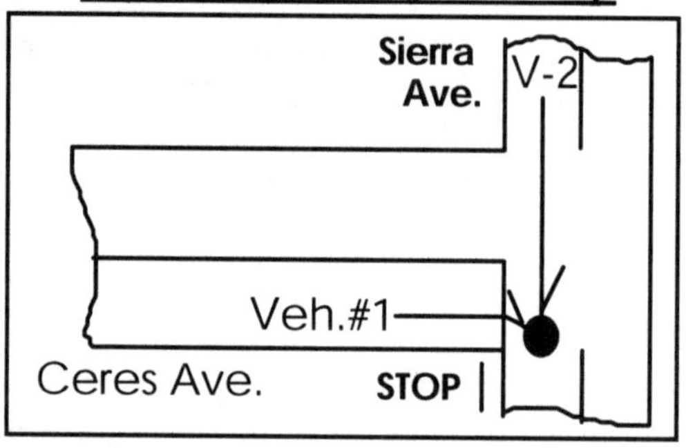

CVC 21801(a) Failure to yield from a stop sign.

Driving left of center

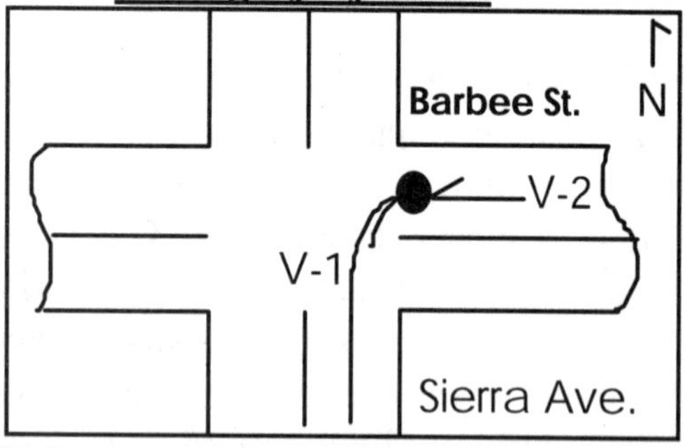

CVC 21650 Veh. makes a right or left turn crossing into the opposing lanes

Failure to yield at a intersection

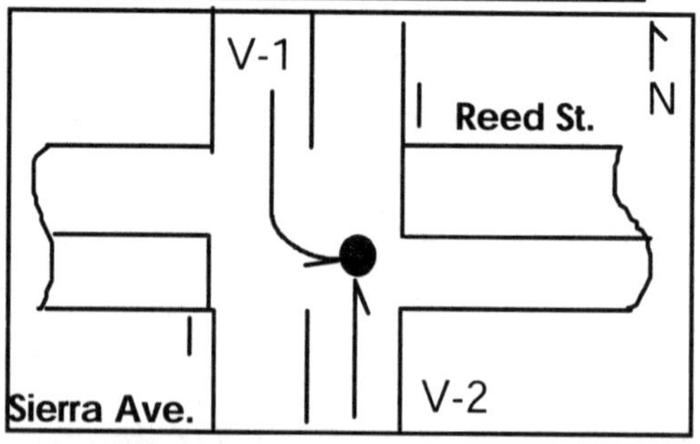

CVC 21801(a) A veh. failing to yield while making a left turn.

Failure to yield from a driveway

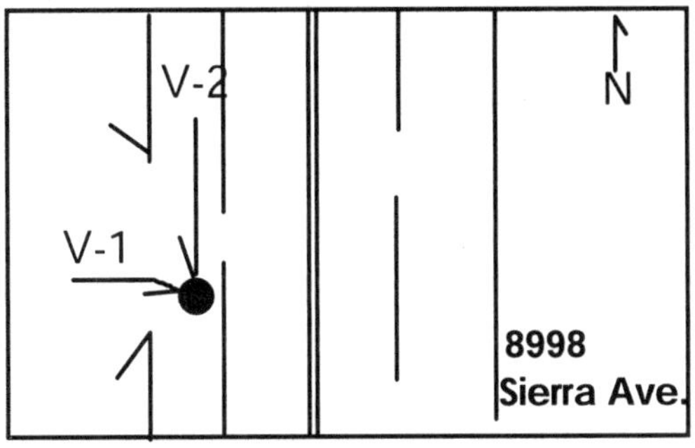

CVC 21804(a) A veh. makes a left or right turn from a private driveway

Lane maneuver

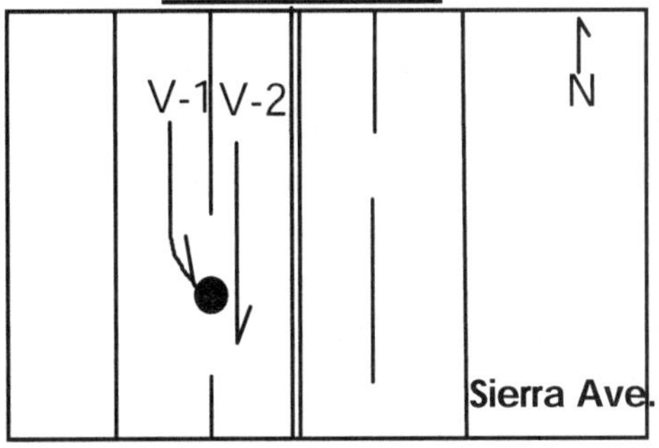

CVC 22107 A veh. attempts a lane change, but strikes an adjacent veh.

Striking a parked vehicle

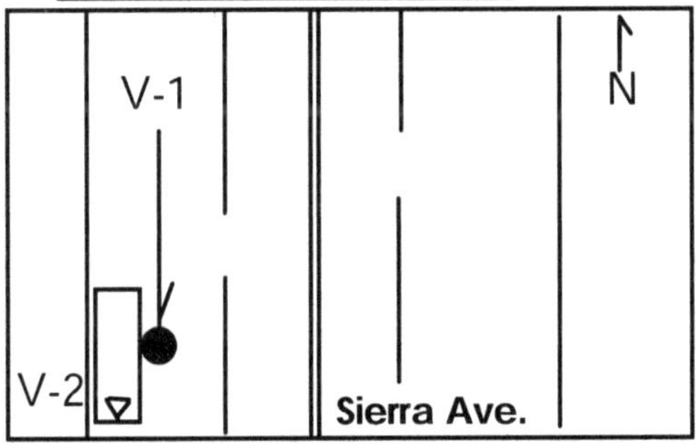

CVC 22107 A vehicle drifts or turns into a parked vehicle

Backing into a parked vehicle

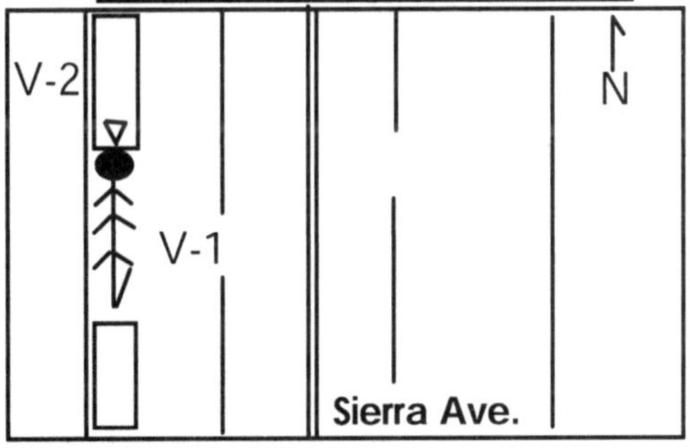

CVC 22106 A veh. strikes a parked vehicle while backing

Making a turn from the wrong lane

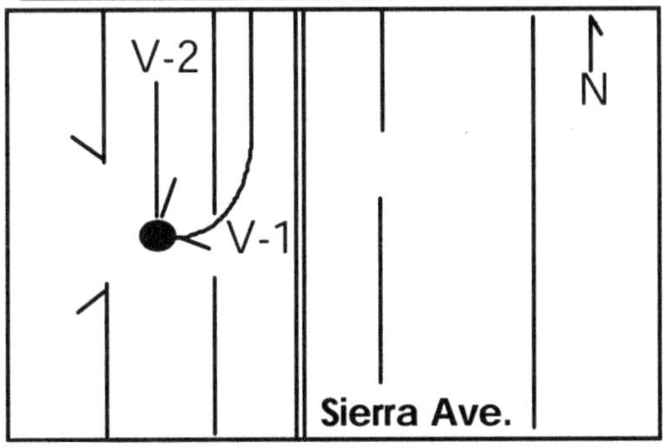

CVC 22100(a) A veh. makes a right turn from the improper position

Failing to stop for a stop sign

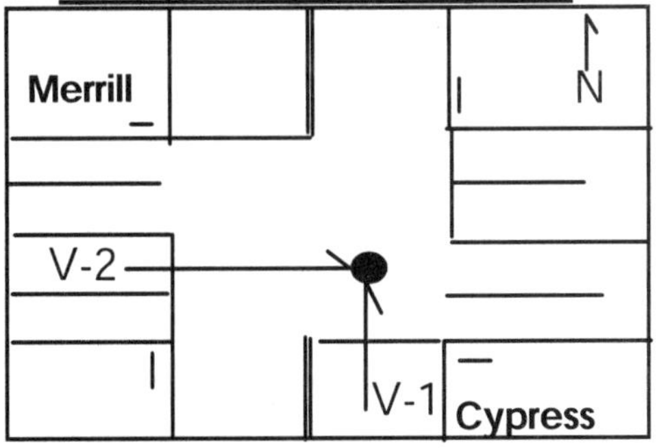

CVC 22450(a) Vehicle #1 failed to stop for the posted stop sign.

SCALE DIAGRAMMING

The scale diagram is a tool which provides the investigating officer with a two dimensional overhead view of the traffic collision scene. The name *factual diagram* is interchangeable with the words *scale diagram* and they are considered one in the same. The factual diagram is a *"snapshot"* of the entire collision scene. Not everything in the scene is reproduced on the factual diagram. Only those items or pieces of evidence that are relevant to the investigation are placed on the diagram. This might include, but is not limited to the following:

- *Vehicle locations and their respective points of rest*
- *Both pre and post impact vehicle skidmarks which show vehicle movement and rotation*
- *Roadway gouges and scrapes*
- *Highway geometric design, e.g. shoulders, landscape, hills, etc*
- *Vehicle debris and fluids*
- *Pedestrian points of rest if they have not been removed from the scene*
- *Overhead lighting and roadway traffic controls*
- *Lane markings, e.g. limit lines and painted traffic control markers*
- *Roadway measurements*
- *Parked vehicles if involved*

DRAWING TOOLS YOU WILL NEED

Basic drafting tools are high on the list of necessary items to complete a factual or scale diagram. These tools do not need be the caliber of professional drafting tools, but your final work product will reflect the quality of tools you have chosen. The following is a list of recommended tools necessary to complete a scale or factual diagram.

Paper:	*Use at least a 8 ½" x 11 stock, preferably a diagram sheet at the rear of the C.H.P. "Injury/Witness" form. This paper has a light grid mark crossing the page that will assist you in the process.*
Pencil:	*A sharp number #2 pencil or automatic "click" style pencil.*
Templates:	*There are several types and styles of templates available on the market. It is a matter of personal preference. The scale should be clear and easy to read. The majority of your diagrams will be drawn in a 1" = 10 feet or 1" = 20 feet scale. Many of the templates are marked with both measurements along the side for easy access. Many of the more commonly used templates can be found in your local uniform stores.*
Compass:	*An inexpensive compass that clamps to your pencil will be adequate.*
French curves:	*These templates come in many shapes and forms. A new product called a "flex curve" is also becoming very popular and will bend to a number of shapes.*
Pencil sharpener:	*This is one of the most basic needs, but is often neglected once the lines begin to widen and become heavy.*
Erasers:	*"Click" style erasers are very handy and allow you to grip the eraser pencil creating a more precision type adjustment.*
Masking tape:	*This is used for anchoring the paper without damaging the surface when it is removed.*
"T" square:	*The "T" square is a tool often used with triangles in drafting. The square combined with the triangles help to speed-up the time needed to draw parallel lines.*
Protractor:	*This tool can be useful in drawing known angles of intersection curb lines.*

Other additional tools are available in many drafting supply stores. Each tool you add to your drawing box will help speed up the entire process. Many traffic collision scenes can take hours, even days to complete. Computer programs such as Visio Draw©, Auto Sketch©, and other traffic related reconstruction programs help you draw the scene if the information is downloaded properly.

GATHERING THE MEASUREMENTS & MARKING THE SCENE

Once the choice of completing a factual diagram is made at a traffic collision scene, the process of marking evidence begins. The evidence you mark will be measured and later transferred to a scale diagram. Earlier I mentioned *walking your scene* when speaking of collision scene analysis. The same walk will allow you to see and mark what is important for the factual diagram.

Marking the scene can be accomplished using a soft crayon-like pencil, or by using some form of *roadway marking paint.* This style of paint is available at your building supply stores. The paint comes in several florescent colors… pink, blue, yellow, red, and green. The spray tip of the paint can limits the area it will cover. This will come in handy for circling a piece of evidence. Maintain several cans of this paint in various colors in a place easy to access quickly.

Decide which color will represent what type of evidence at the scene. For example, you could use blue paint for skidmarks. Then, if you were to use a color like red for vehicle markings you'll see a strong contrast with the blue skidmarks. Other mentioned colors may be used for marking vehicle debris or property relevant to the accident scene. Be flexible when choosing your colors for marking both evidence and vehicles. Many collisions represent a strong challenge when the skidmarks cross each other several times.

Roadway paint will also remain on the roadway many days and weeks after the accident has been investigated. This will allow you to return to the scene to check your diagram and measurements against those still visible. Some officers like to mark the roadway immediately just in case it's learned that a diagram is needed after all. It's too late after the vehicles and evidence are moved.

There are many ways of marking a scene for later measurement gathering. There is no hard and fast rule for marking a tire or circling a piece of important evidence. The use of these marking tools is up to you. We will discuss the basics of this principle and encourage you to develop your own style in this process.

Vehicles & Tires: Mark all four tires of any vehicle you plan to document. This will give you latitude when deciding which three of the measurements appears to be the easiest to gather at the time.

Use your paint to make a "T" in front of the tire as follows.

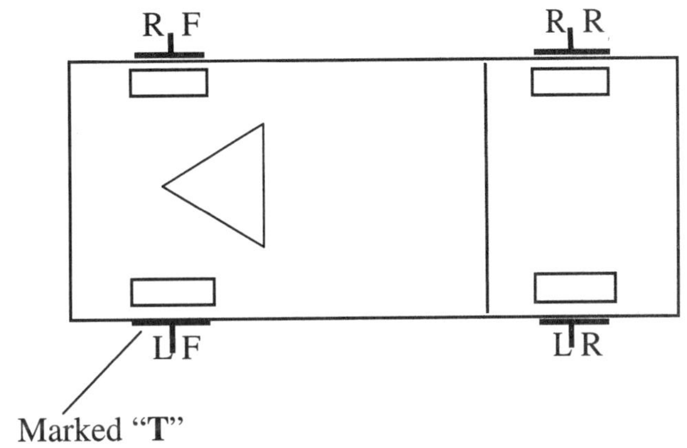

Vehicle Debris: Vehicle debris both in the roadway and on the surrounding ground may be circled using your roadway marking paint. The paint works well for dirt, grass and other surfaces. Make a wide circle around the object without spray painting the object itself.

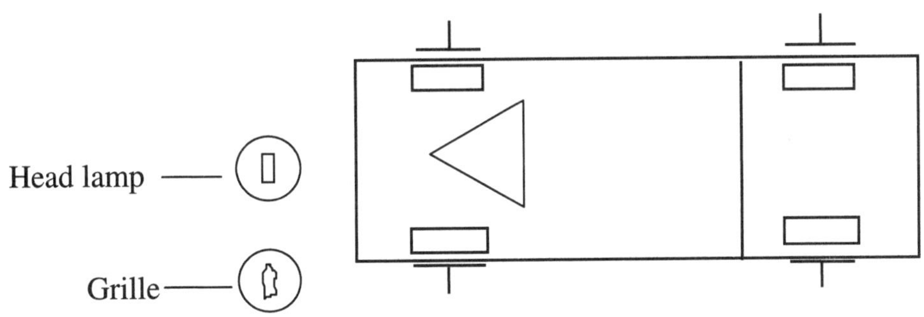

***Skidmarks*:** Skidmarks can be easy or hard to document depending on the number and pattern of the marks themselves. Stand back at the beginning of the skidmark, and look toward the direction of the accident scene. Don't forget to confirm the skidmark is relevant to this collision. Make a *"U"* shaped mark at the beginning of the mark. While walking the skidmark paint a line on either side of the mark at various points until you reach the tire or the end of the "skid" itself. Once this is completed, return to the beginning of the skid and *"Dot"* the skid at your measurement points. The lines outside of the mark will assist you in visualizing the progression of the skid into the accident scene.

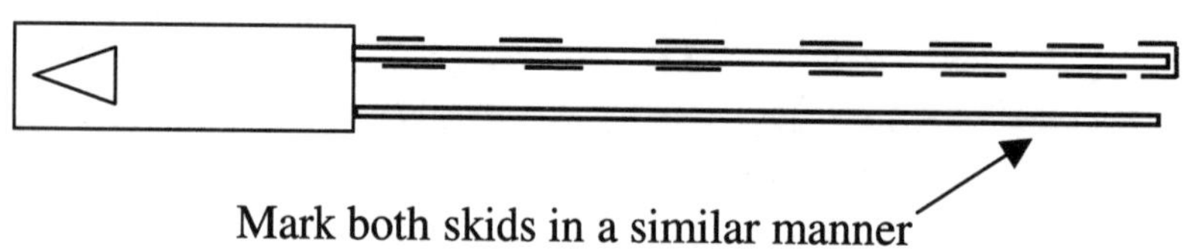

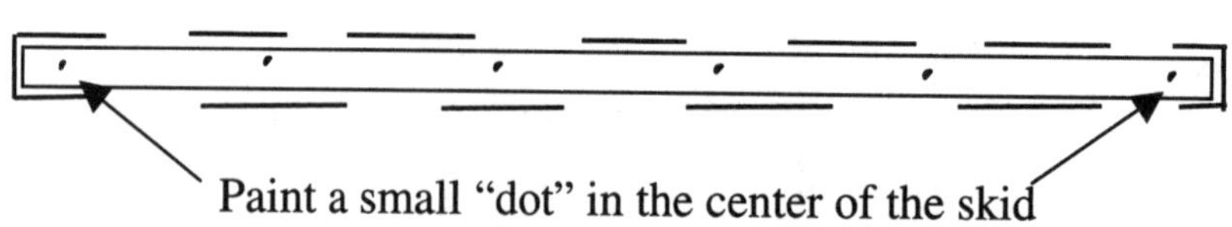

***Pedestrians*:** If the pedestrian remains at the scene due to being fatally injured in the collision, we will also need to mark the location of the body. We will not however be marking the deceased in the same manner as the television and movie industry. Five marks will be used to preserve the position of the victim. The feet, hands, and head will be marked using a *discrete* amount of paint. Use extra care not to spray the body itself.

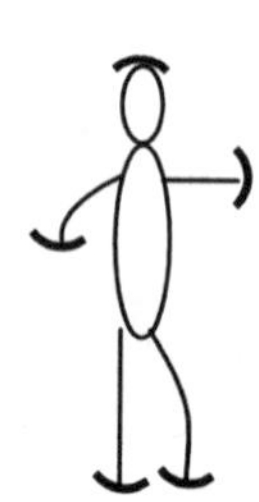

***Other items*:** Other items will be present at the scene which will be marked in a similar way. Loose tires, vehicle parts, and important items will need to be marked and measured. Use a small amount of paint, remembering anything you mark will visibly clutter the scene during the photography segment of your investigation.

MEASURING TOOLS

Tools for measuring the collision scene play a very important part in the later reproduction of the same scene. The measurements you make at the accident location must be accurate or the diagram you will be drawing may not reflect the true appearance of the scene. Earlier in this book, we talked about having a *collision kit*. This might simply be an area where you store the tools necessary to collect your crime scene evidence and maintain your measuring and marking tools. Check this area often and ensure it has been stocked properly. Once on scene, a run back to the station may waste important time in processing the incident. Here's a suggested list of useful items to keep in your *collision scene response kit.*

***Steel and fiber glass tapes*:** These tapes can be purchased in various lengths and stored in a small area. The fiberglass tapes should be easy to read and have a roll-up mechanism. The end should have a small hook to be fastened to the ground with a pavement nail. *200'* and *300'* lengths are preferable.

***Pavement nails*:** These nails will secure the fiberglass tapes in place as they are stretched out to their full length across the roadway.

***Hammer*:** The hammer will both pound in the pavement nails and serve to remove them as well. The hammer should be small, but able to do the job.

***Level*:** Levels are available in *"percentages of grade"* and will provide the investigator with the grade either approaching or leaving the scene. This will become important in later skidmark analysis.

***Flashlight*:** Carry an extra fully charged flashlight with your kit. The measurement process can be extensive, and will quickly discharge your duty flashlight. Many cities have purchased portable lighting that will greatly assist you in this area.

***Pad and paper*:** Keep a fresh tablet of paper in your response kit. Notes taken at the scene and measurements can be kept in one place utilizing this system.

REFERENCE LINE & REFERENCE POINT

This measuring system is one of the more widely used of the many forms of documenting a collision scene. Many other ways of measuring crime scenes are available, such as triangulation, but this form of measurement has proven to be one of the most reliable and easiest methods. The reference line and reference point method simply put is a *coordinate system.* Many of you remember the number line from your early elementary school days. The coordinate system is a set of two number lines. One of these lines is placed in a *horizontal direction,* with the other being placed in a *vertical direction.* The horizontal and vertical lines are placed on a *two-dimensional flat surface.*

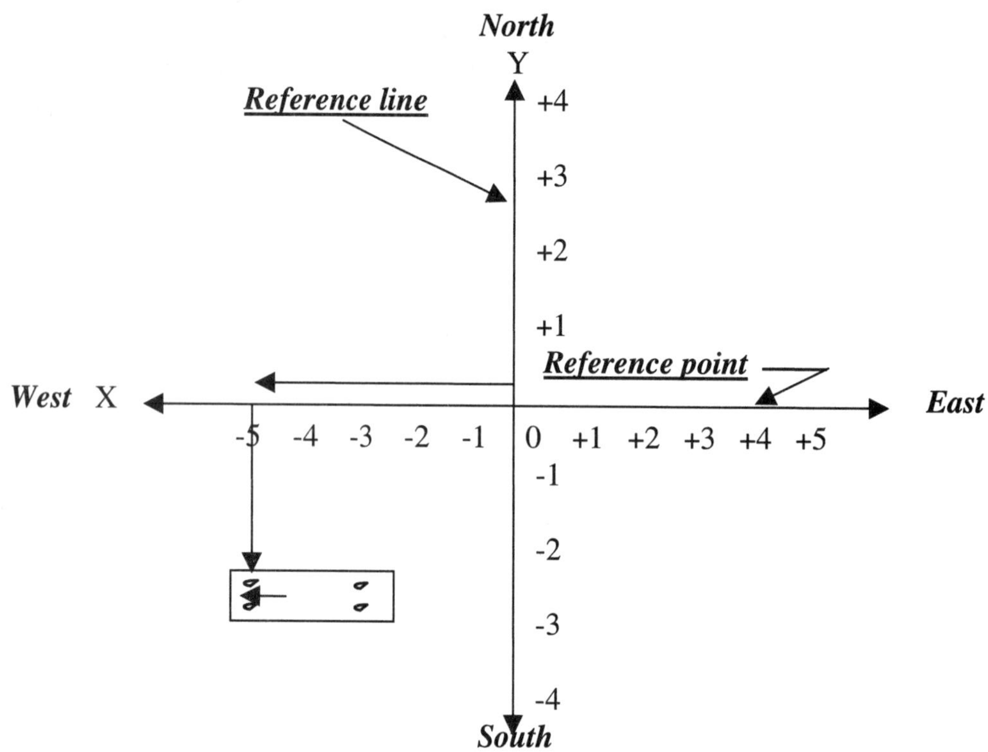

Geometry teachers refer to this system as the *"X, Y and Z"* coordinate measuring system. The *"Z axis"* is used to measure height on a *three dimensional plane.* For the purposes of this book and basic accident investigation, we will be using the *X and Y system* only. The *X and Y* axis coordinate measuring method utilizes a *positive* and *negative* counting system. The graph can be modified to suit the needs of the accident investigator. We will be replacing the *X* and *Y* letters with the names *"Reference Point"* and *"Reference Line"* respectively. The remainder of the information on the graph will remain essentially the same. The easiest way of demonstrating this measurement system is to use the above graph.

Each point on the coordinate system is measured from *two* different directions on the graph. The first measurement is taken from the *reference line*, with the second measurement taken from the *reference point.* The graph shows the front right tire of vehicle #1 was measured in the *minus* direction on the *X*-axis, and the *minus* direction of the *Y*-axis. To simplify the measurements, we can substitute the directions of *North, South, East, and West* for the plus and minus side of our graph. The plus and minus may then be removed from the graph with a positive measurement in each of the four directions. By removing the positive and negative type measurements, we may avoid a mistake in the documentation process. Each type of measurement is appropriate, and either will be acceptable.

True direction measurement

- ***Right front tire*** ***5.25 feet w/of the R/L & 2.25 feet s/of the R/P***

Plus and minus measurement

- ***Right front tire*** ***-5.25 feet from the R/L & -2.25 feet from the R/P***

The example above compares both the *"True Direction"* method and *"Plus and Minus"* measurements. As you can see, the true direction measurement system appears to be the least complicated method of the two and provides less chance for error. The graph depicted on the previous page may be adjusted in any of the four directions to facilitate the best use of the coordinate system. Rather than measure both plus and minus in all four directions, we can place the *X and Y* axis over the accident scene in such a way as to keep the measurements in one of the four quadrants of the system. More simply speaking, the *reference point* and line should be chosen to expedite the measurement process.

All evidence, involved vehicles and skidmarks will be measured from these lines. By isolating the evidence into one of the four quadrants, the steel measuring tapes will remain in one place with a minimum of movement. The steel tape is nailed into the roadway and essentially becomes the center of the graph where the lines would cross. Accidents do however occur where the *reference line* cannot be placed in such a way as to isolate the evidence. The steel tape will be nailed into the ground, and this will allow for a reversal of the tape in the opposite direction without losing the location of your original *reference point.* The example on the following page will demonstrate the process of quadrant isolation utilizing an intersection curb line prolongation as the *reference point.*

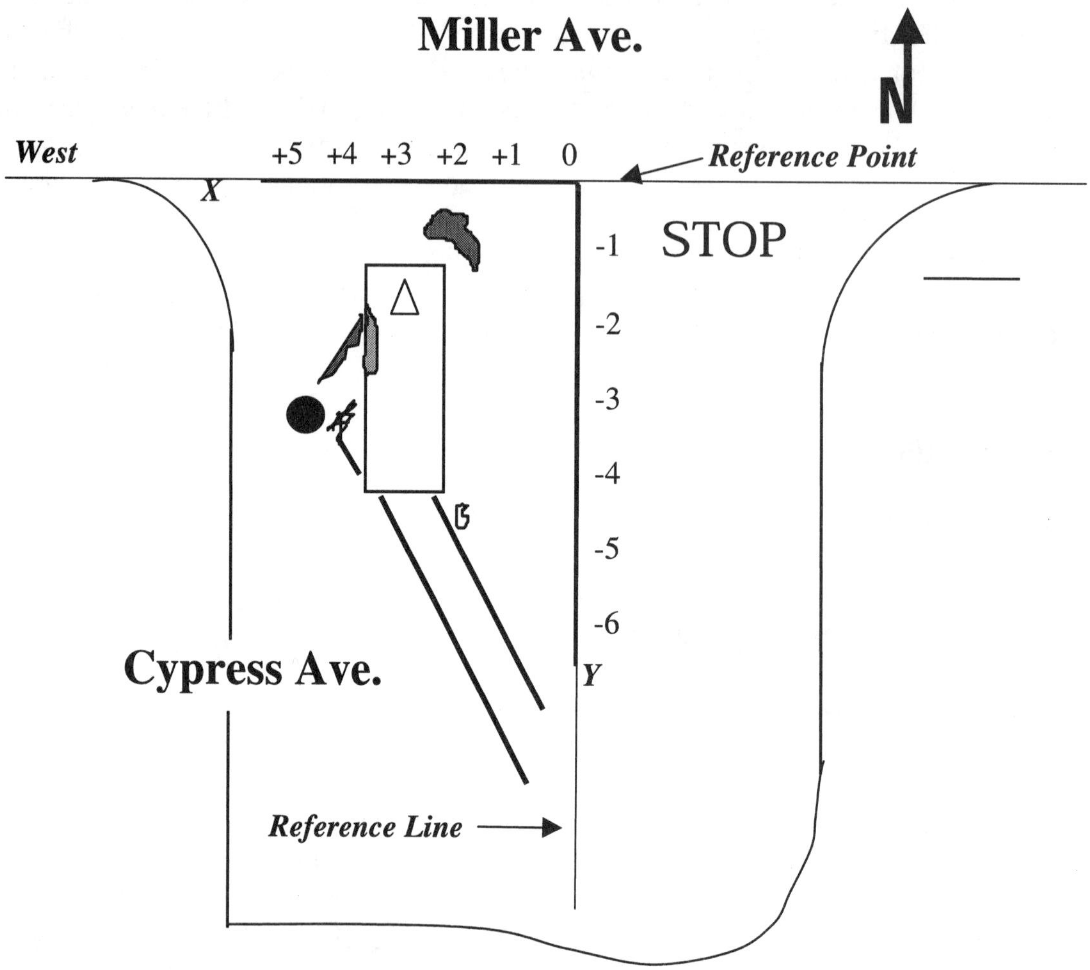

Rather than extending the *X and Y-axis* in a direction not necessary, we have limited the need for additional measuring tapes and traffic control.

REFERENCE LINE & REFERENCE POINT

Selecting the location of the *reference line* and *reference point* is up to you. The roadway edge can be used as one of the points. However, this would make measuring from the edge difficult. Choose one of the roadway lane markers as your *reference line* if at all possible. This is somewhat of a natural straight line which will assist you in keeping the *reference line* and *reference point* at a *90-degree* angle. The *reference point* may be placed at the extension of one of the roadway curb lines. This is also commonly referred to as the *prolongation line*. This may not always be an easy task. Collisions occur on and off of the roadway. A permanent marker such as a telephone or electric pole will serve as a fixed object in which to align your *reference point*. A majority of the telephone and electrical poles have a *numbered steel plate* attached to it. Extend an imaginary line of sight from the pole to the lane line in the roadway where your point will be placed or nailed into the pavement.

The diagram below demonstrates the measurement process at the scene. However, the actual measurements are not placed on the diagram, but rather in the body of your report, under the heading *"measurements."*

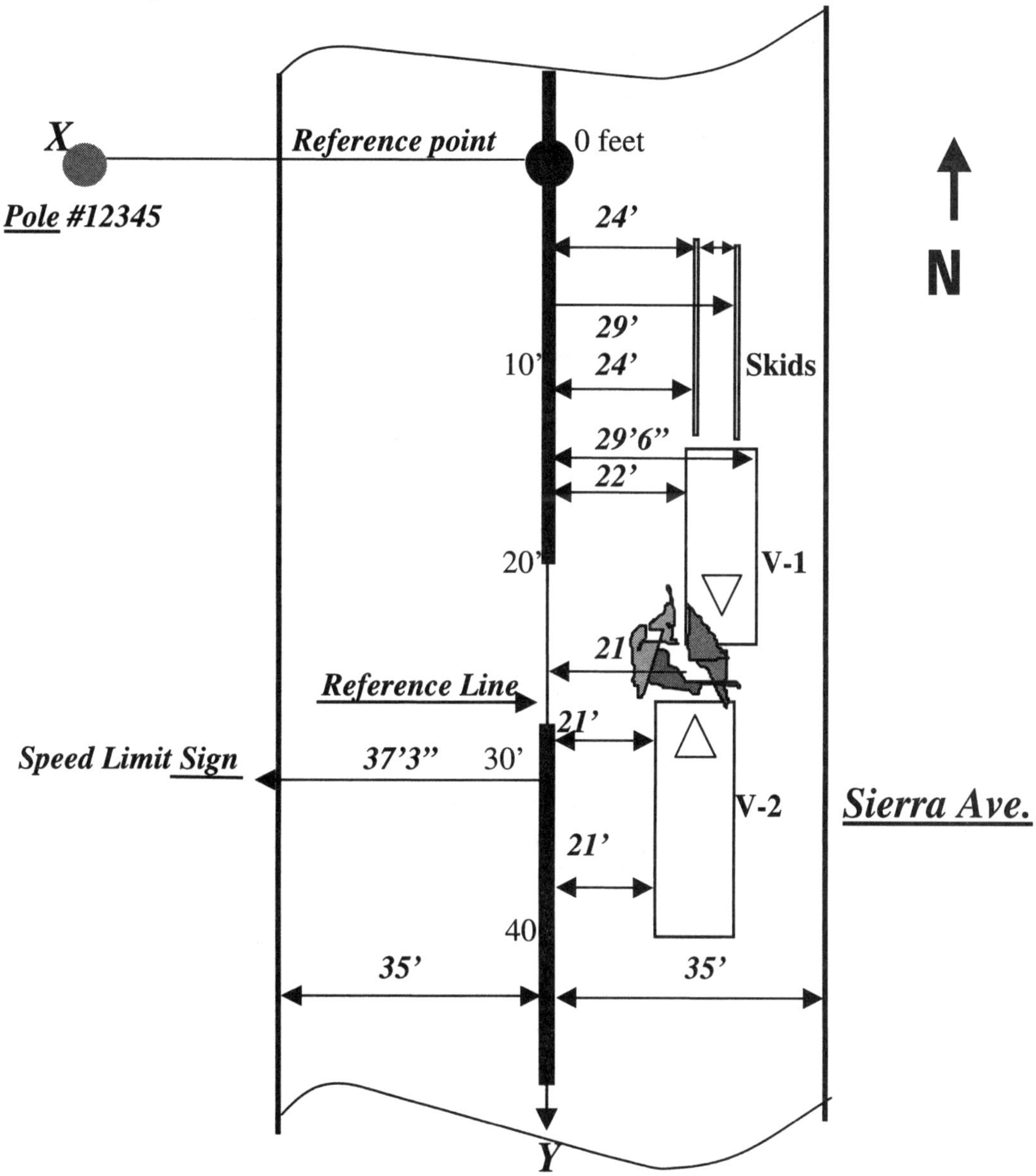

In the above example, the measurements were taken from a fixed telephone pole on the West Side of Sierra Ave. An imaginary line was extended eastbound from the pole toward the center of the roadway. Once at the lane markers, a fiberglass tape was stretched south along the lane line and nailed into the pavement at the point where the lane marker makes a *90-degree* angle with the prolongation of the pole. In this case all of the vehicle and evidence measurements have been isolated in the southeast quadrant of the *X and Y-axis* we spoke of earlier. The measurements may be taken one by one utilizing this system. Roadway measurements, street signs, and traffic direction signals may all be measured using this system.

NO measurement to the reference line or *reference point* is necessary. The entire intersection and scene will be measured out from the point that you select. To demonstrate this process, the reference point and *reference line* can be placed anywhere in the scene as long as the point and line make a 90-degree angle with one another. The purpose of using a lane line or street prolongation is to aid in the *line of sight* when picking a straight line. Diagramming from a random selected point will be covered later in this chapter.

CURVES

The examples depicted in the previous pages will assist you in picking your reference line and reference point in the majority of cases. Many collisions however occur on a curved roadway well away from the more easily measured streets of the city. For this reason, we must adapt our documentation methods to assist us in this scenario. Roadway curves present a different challenge in measuring for a factual diagram. There are two methods of measuring a roadway curve and vehicle information.

The first of these two methods utilizes the techniques we put into motion in the coordinate system.

- Check the curve for a point in which it meets a straight portion of the roadway. If this type of curve is present, extend the *reference line* from the *prolongation* of the straight portion of the roadway toward the curve.

- Once this is accomplished, the *reference point* may be extended across the beginning of the curve where it meets the straight roadway making a 90-degree angle for the two points.

- After the tapes are in place, the measurements may be taken from these two lines toward the vehicle or object in which you intend to document.

The *reference line* and the *reference points* may be rotated in such a way as to facilitate the gathering of this information. The *reference point* may be placed across the bottom of the curve as long as a 90-degree angle is made with the *reference line*. The following two examples demonstrate this *line and point placement* on the curved roadway.

Top Placement

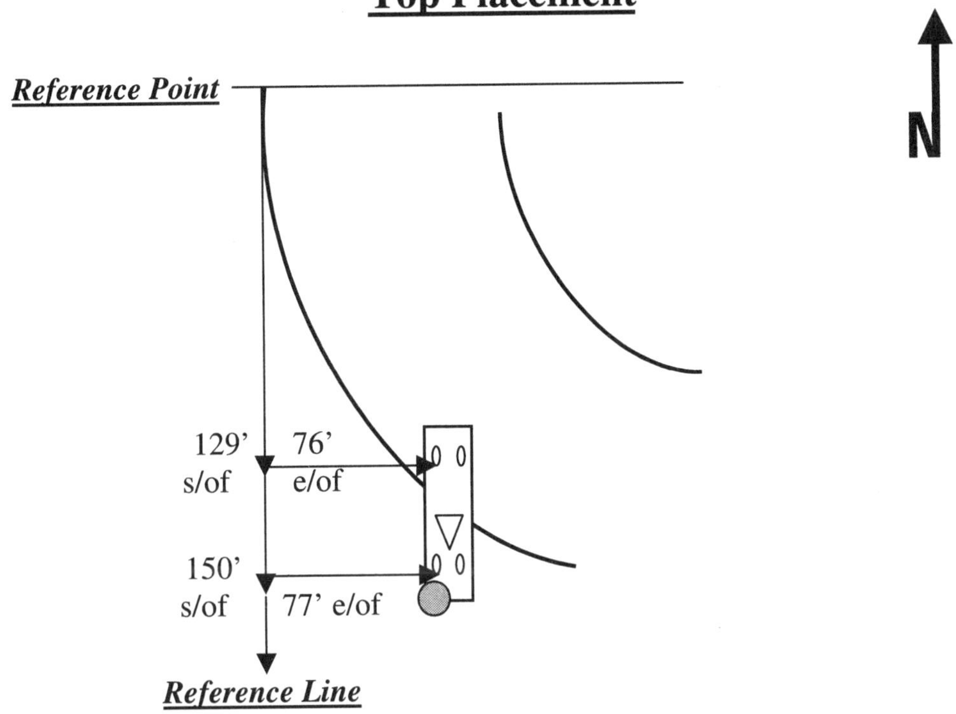

The Reference Line and Reference Point method may also be used to measure the curve itself as demonstrated in the adjacent diagrams.

Bottom Placement

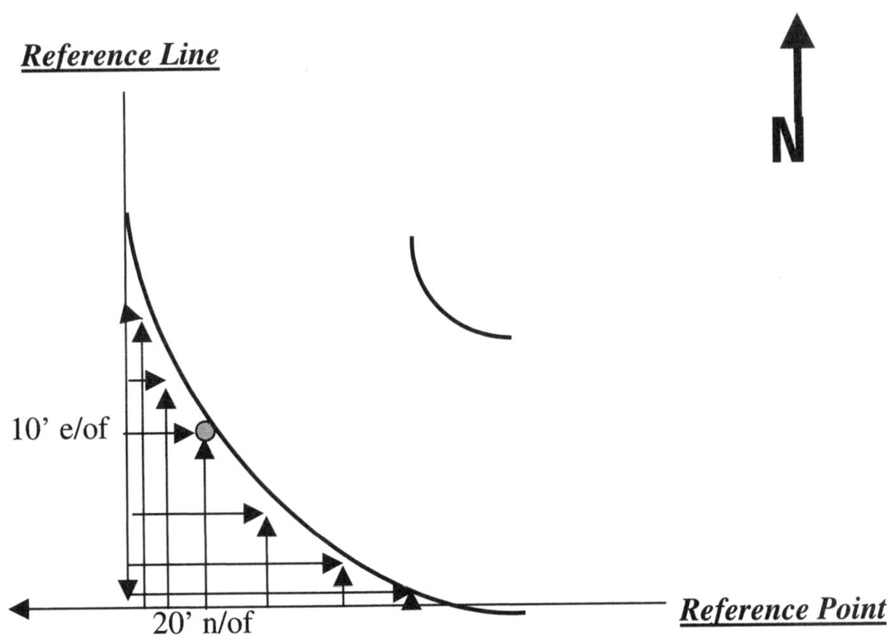

Triangulation provides a secondary method of measuring a curve of the roadway and can be an alternate to the *reference line* or *point* method. The advantage of this method will become clear if obstacles, such as houses, buildings, or trees, exist outside of the roadway. Triangulation allows the investigator to remain within the roadway while gathering measurements. When looking at a curve, you will notice the inside of the curve is by far, a shorter distance. In the *triangulation method*, we will be measuring then drawing a series of imaginary *triangles* on the roadway with measuring tapes. These triangles will be reproduced on your diagram sheets in a much smaller scale. Mark the inside of the curve at a interval of *ten feet* using a roadway marking paint. The outside or larger area of the curve can be marked every *twenty feet*. This difference in marking will account for the larger and smaller portions of the curve and can be adjusted depending on the size of the area covered. Once the inside and outside of the curve is marked, measure and document the remaining *two* measurements which cross between the known points.

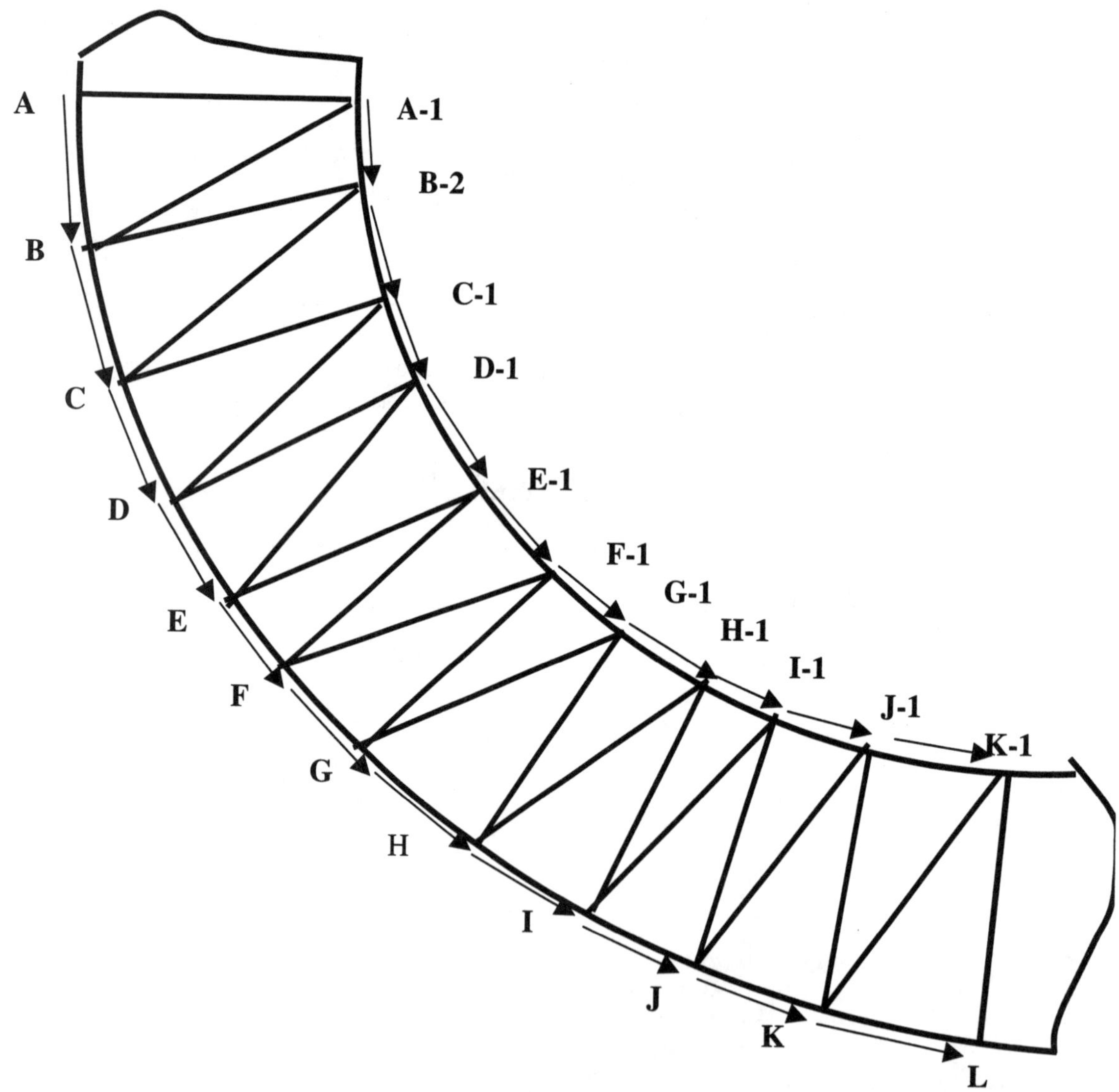

WHAT ABOUT CORNERS OF THE INTERSECTION?

Many of the intersections you encounter will not meet one another for 90-degree angles. For this reason, you will need to measure the corners and then solve a mathematical formula. Each corner of an intersection is, in effect, *one quarter of a full circle*. You're faced with measuring in a manner to determine the radius of a curve. The radius of the curve can be measured using the same tools as we used to measure a intersection. *Two steel tapes* are all that is necessary for this venture. Once the measurements are obtained, we can use the mathematical formula below, which, once solved, will determine the radius of the corner or curve.

Radius Formula:

$$r = \frac{C^2}{8m} + \frac{m}{2}$$

In the above formula, *"r"* represents *radius, "C"* represents *chord,* and *"m"* represents the *"middle ordinate."* Radius of the curve is what we are solving for, therefore, we must obtain the *chord,* and *middle ordinate* measurements. Once these measurements have been taken, we will return to the formula and plug them in.

Intersection

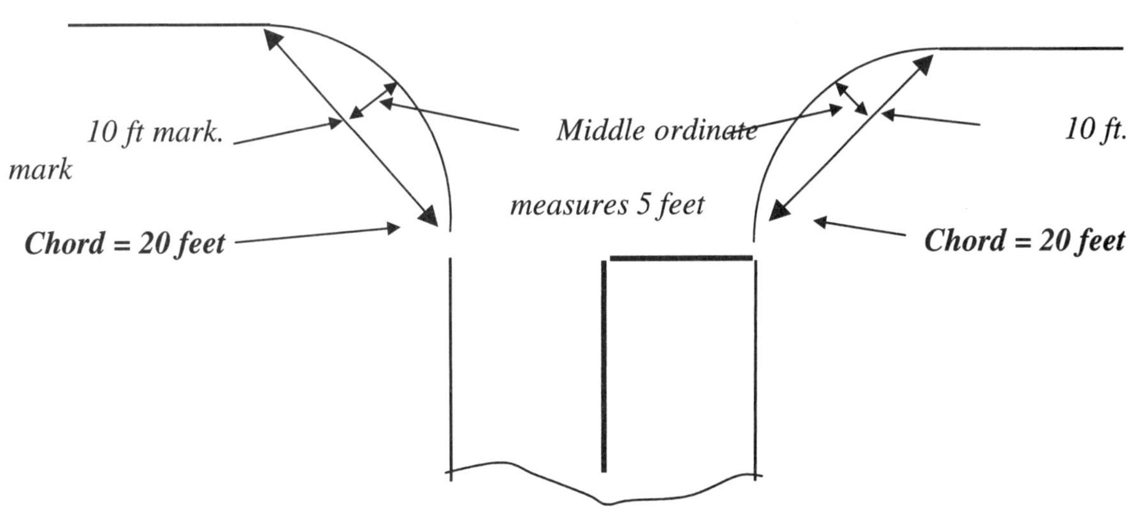

The *chord* is a measurement obtained by stretching a steel tape from the point where the curve begins and the point where the curve begins to straighten again. In the example above, the *chord* was found to measure *20 feet*. Locate the point on the *cord* measurement that is *½ the total length of the chord*. In this case 10 feet. The second steel tape should be placed at a *90-degree angle* to this *halfway point on the cord*. The *90-*

degree angle is very important, or the secondary measurement will not be accurately obtained. For this example the *cord* measurement was *20 feet*, therefore the *middle ordinate* measurement will be taken at the *10 foot* mark on the *chord.*

The *middle ordinate* will be the next measurement taken in this exercise. Stretch the second tape measure toward the curve from the *chord* at a 90-degree angle. The *middle ordinate* measurement will be marked at the point where the second tape meets the curve. For this example, the *middle ordinate* measured *5 feet.* These measurements may then be placed into the formula discussed on the previous page.

Chord = ***20 feet***
Middle ordinate = ***5 feet***
Radius = ***unknown***

$$r = \frac{C^2}{8m} + \frac{m}{2}$$

or

$$r = \frac{(20')^2}{8(5')} + \frac{(5')}{2}$$

or

$$r = \frac{(400)}{(40')} + \frac{(5')}{2}$$

or

$$r = 10 + 2.5 \longrightarrow 12.5'$$

The radius equals ⟶ ***12' 6 inches***

All measurements are in *tenths* and must be converted into *inches.*

The majority of corners at one intersection in your city will all be the same. If you measure one of the corners, you do not need to repeat this process on each and every corner. Quickly check the measurements of one corner with the measurement of another similar corner. Also, don't become frustrated if the measurements and calculations are not exact. Remember the cement or asphalt is being poured and shaped using a human element. The chances of the corner having an *exact* even radius will be very rare. Mistakes can also be made in *eye-balling* where the curve begins and ends.

Many of the original radius measurements are maintained in the civil engineering divisions of your city halls. Occasionally radius measurements are all but impossible to obtain due to walls or structures that have been built at the intersection. Remember, there is a great likelihood that all four corners of the intersection have the same radius.

TRACKING YOUR MEASUREMENTS

Tracking your measurements in a sequential order may save you a great deal of headaches and frustration later in the diagramming process. Accurate measuring and documentation will keep the investigating officer from returning to the scene due to lost, misplaced, or merely sloppy notes. Several ways of tracking your measurements have been developed for your use. The majority of these forms are simple to obtain or create on a computer. However, the measurements may also be maintained on a tablet of paper at the scene. The following form is easy to develop and is commonly used by accident investigators.

Reference Point		*Reference Line*
1. L/F Tire 27' s/of	*&*	*18'7" e/of*
2. L/R Tire 45' s/of	*&*	*18' e/of*

This is a small example of the measurement documentation form, which may be used at a collision scene. The amount of forms used is clearly dependent on the amount of measurements you intend to gather. A large scene may have up to *200 - 300* or more measurements. A clear concise record of each measurement will be less confusing to the officer completing the diagram. A properly documented scene can be an invaluable tool to the *Traffic Collision Reconstructionist.* Skidmarks may be measured and verified strictly by the measurement sheets attached to the rear of your reports. Those officers who plan to create a sheet similar to diagram above may wish to carry these in their collision response kit. Once organized, these same measurements can be added to your investigative reports.

RECREATING THE SCENE ON PAPER

The scene has been cleared, and you now face the task of recreating the scene on paper. Prepare yourself for this task by locating a comfortable location in which to complete your diagram. This may include a desk, large table, or a drafting board if one is available to you. Take the time to look over all of your measurements, photos, and any relevant other information which will help you to complete this project. This review process will refresh your memory about the curb lines, lane markings, and other important diagram items.

Whether you choose to use the C.H.P. diagram sheets, or a large piece of drawing paper, plan for the scale which you intend to use when drawing your scene. The two most common scales used are the *1" equals 10 feet* and *1" equals 20 feet.* Either scale is acceptable, however the larger the scale, the larger the paper you must choose to finish your drawing. The C.H.P. forms may be taped together end to end rather than using one large piece of drafting paper. Drafting paper, unlike the smaller C.H.P. forms, must be folded later and attached to the main report.

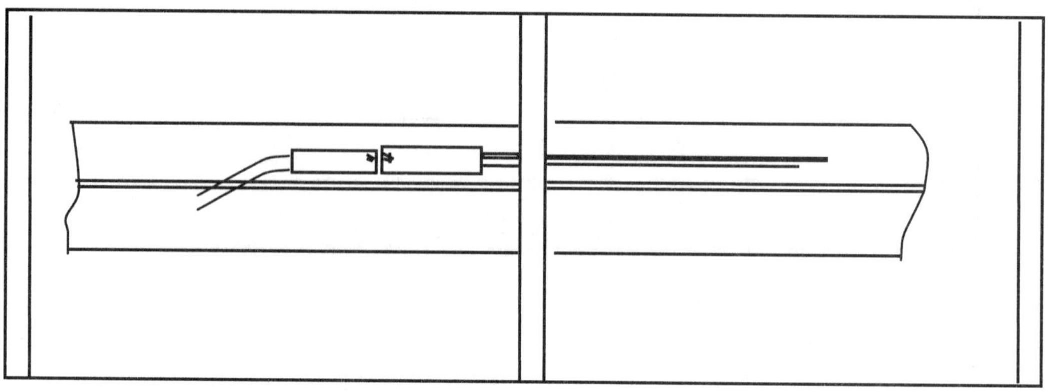

The above example demonstrates the combined use of two C.H.P 556 forms to draw one collision scene. Be sure to plan the location where the majority of your evidence will be located on this type of diagram. The overall length of your scene will be known at the conclusion of gathering your measurements. Take the longest measurement and place it over the taped sheets of paper. This will help you to visualize how the scene will fit on your paper. Try not to become frustrated while picturing the scene, as this takes time to complete. This process will become much easier for you the more you draw.

REFERENCE LINE & REFERENCE POINT OF THE DIAGRAM

Reference lines and *reference points* are used only as a guide on the final factual diagram. Draw a light line on the paper in the same position as the reference lines and reference point was placed on the street. Again the questions arises, *"Why did we not measure the reference line and reference point from the curb edges?"* Remember the intersection is measured out from the *reference point* and *reference line*, and not vice versa. This can best be demonstrated by placing a *point* anywhere on the paper and starting your measurements from this point. The roadway widths and basic intersection should begin to take shape as if they were all measured from this point at the scene.

If this sounds confusing, try drawing your *reference line* and *reference point* on a blank piece of paper before trying the full diagram. This will help you visualize the entire intersection and how it should be placed in the final draft. Drawing the intersection is the first order of business in finishing the basics of the diagram. Once the point is placed, measure out to where the roadway edges should be drawn. From the reference point and reference line, draw a parallel line towards the opposite end of the paper that reflects the roadway width. Draw your lane lines if necessary, and move on to the roadway corners using the radius formula demonstrated in the earlier pages.

The corners of the intersection can be re-created using the radius formula we discussed earlier. Once the formula has been solved, the answer found will become the radius used in the diagram. Most of diagram templates on the market have several radius curves in the appropriate scale already cut into them for easier reproduction. Look for the radius in the *same scale* as your diagram and align the curve with your drawn edge lines. Complete your curve lightly and allow for possible adjustments if necessary. If your radius formula gives you an answer very close to one of the template curves, chances are your measurements or the design of the intersection are slightly off. The decision is yours whether to use the closest radius match or to draw the radius using your drafting tools. If you choose to draw the curve using a compass, follow the steps bellow:

RADIUS EXAMPLE USING YOUR COMPASS

Your diagram has begun to take shape, but drawing the appropriate scale corners with a template cannot be accomplished. The formula used previously can be utilized to solve for the scale radius measurement. The answer however, may not match closely to the available scale drawings in many of the templates. For this reason, you may choose to draw the corners with your compass. The first step will be to extend light lines making a 90-degree angle at your corner. This will be the point where your compass will first be placed. We must first gain the needed radius measurement to draw the corner. Solve the radius formula first, and you will use this answer in your diagram process. Use the same scale for the radius as you did in the other part of your diagram. *Do not make the mistake* of using a *1 inch = 10 feet radius* on a *1 inch = 20 foot diagram.* Many officers will draw a radius utilizing a template that displays radius curves in both scale measurements causing the diagram to misrepresent the true proportions of the intersection.

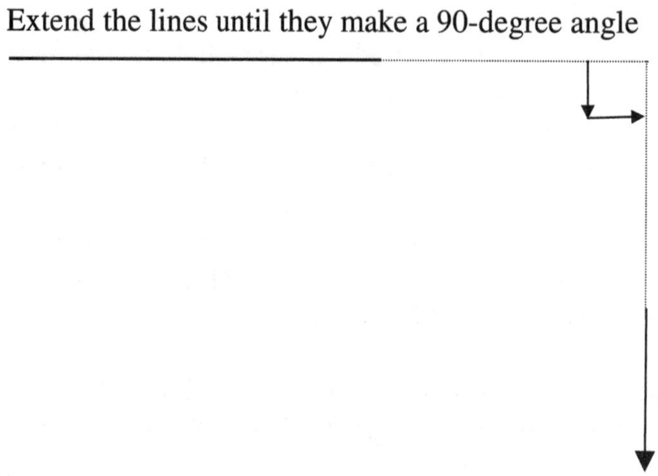

Use the answer from the radius equation and extend the compass to match this measurement on the appropriate scale. For example, the radius measurement on the previous page was found to be *12.5 feet*. Place the metal point of the compass at *zero* on the template and extend the pencil portion of the compass to *12.5 feet or 12 feet 6 inches.* Remember, the radius formula will provide us with a answer in 10ths, not 12ths as required in our measuring system.

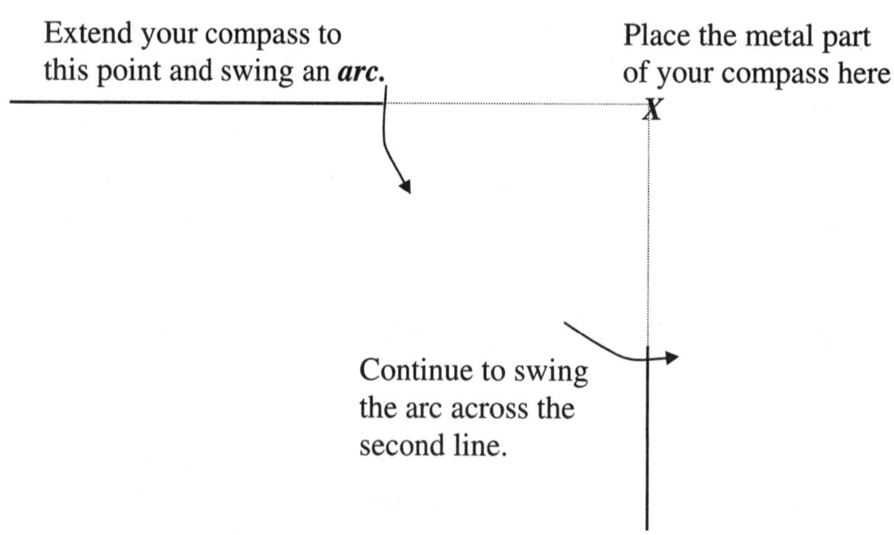

The first two *arcs* have been created on the main curb lines utilizing this process. The metal compass point is now moved and placed on the new pivot points that were drawn by our first two arcs. Swing *two* more *arcs* toward the center of the square. You will soon see the two new *arcs* have crossed creating a *third* and final *pivot point*. Place the metal portion of your compass on this newly drawn pivot point. This third point will allow the pencil portion of the compass to swing the *radius* from curve to curve, connecting the points.

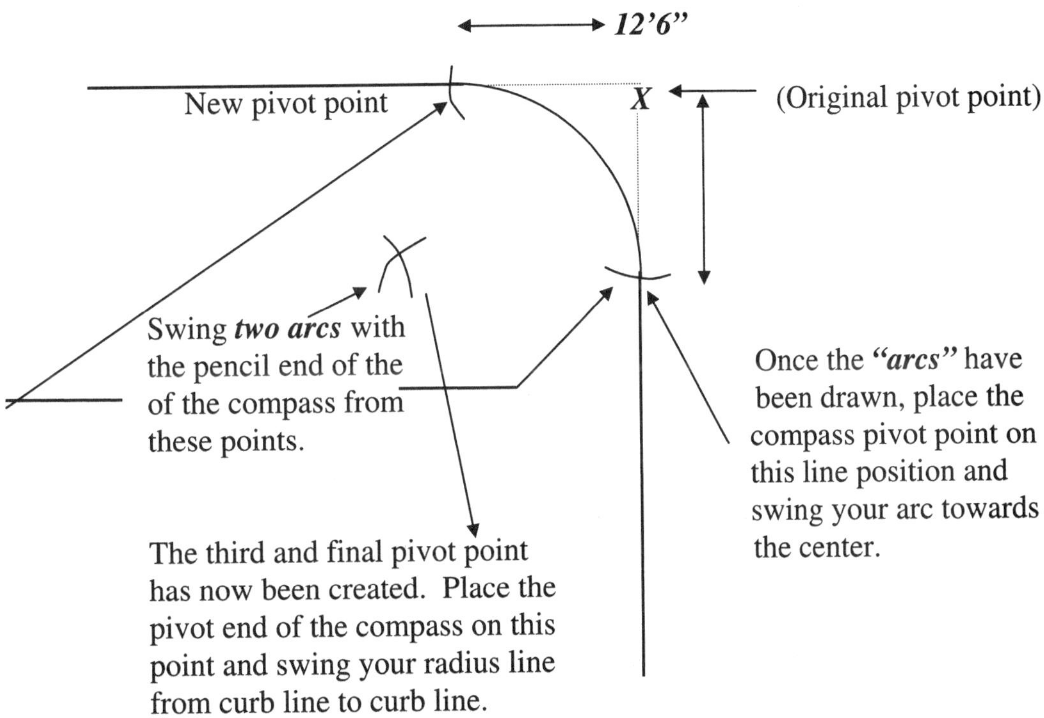

STARTING TO TAKE SHAPE

You have completed the roadway edges, shoulder, and any other outside points of importance. The roadway is beginning to take shape. This first step outlined above will help you visualize your final product. Take a break in your work, and check your measurements against the notes you took at the scene. Do the roadway widths and do lane lines appear to match closely with the rough sketch you drew at the scene? This is the time for changes if they need to be done. Once the vehicles and evidence has been placed on the diagram, it will be difficult to change the overall look of the drawing without appearing sloppy.

Everything appears to match the measurements you took earlier. Now is the time to place your involved vehicles on the diagram. Each of the vehicles should have *three* tire measurements. This will give you the shape necessary to draw the vehicle in proper proportion. The C.H.P. templates have rectangular vehicle's shapes already cut into them for tracing. Draw the oval shaped tires first at your measurement points, and find the right vehicle shape to draw over them. Remember that the tire measurement is not the total length of the vehicle. A rectangular shape over the tires is necessary to show vehicle proportion.

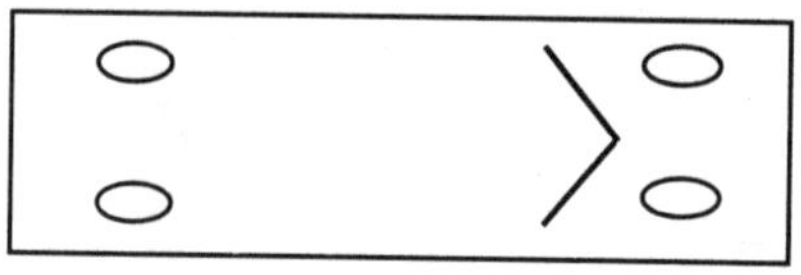

Other vehicles such as large vans, buses and trains will be drawn using a template or by free hand. You may also wish to combine a shape from several different templates to complete the vehicle type for which you are looking for.

Other items such as vehicle debris, fluids, and skidmarks may be added after the initial drawing starts to take shape. The majority of the items drawn on your factual diagram can be found on templates which are readily available on the market. Skidmarks should be added using the measurements taken at the scene. The width of the marks should be reasonably accurate, but does not need to be exact. Place your points on the diagram, and draw parallel lines on either side of the marks. The skidmarks will begin to take shape. Try to use a pencil which will duplicate the darkness and density of the actual marks as you remember them.

TREES, SHRUBS, & FENCES

Add trees, shrubs, and fences at the very end of the drawing process. These items are the finishing touches on the factual diagram and give the drawing depth. Try to draw only those additional items that are necessary in the presentation process. A diagram can become cluttered with too much outside information. This can distract the observer from the true focus of your drawing.

LEGEND

The legend in a factual diagram is not required, but it is suggested depending on the number of items that need reference. A factual diagram can become cluttered with additional information such as evidence, vehicle debris, and any other relevant items. You must make the decision as to how much information needs to be addressed on the diagram. If references to evidence are limited, you may chose to add them adjacent to the objects. If the amount of information is substantial, a legend will become essential.

Number or label each piece of evidence on the factual diagram with either a *number* or *letter*. Add an additional page to the back of the diagramming area, and explain each one of the corresponding references on the drawing. This process will help to keep your diagram neat and easy to read.

THE FINAL REVIEW

The factual diagram has been completed and is ready to add at the end of the original report. Take a few minutes to review your work. Match the Polaroid® photos to the diagram and see if they appear to be accurate. Do the vehicles look proportional for the roadway size and shape? Have you labeled your streets and added all of the area traffic controls? Do each of your numbers or letters on the legend match the corresponding numbers on the diagram? Once the copies of the report have been made, you cannot go back and change any portion of the report including the factual diagram.

The factual diagram process can be a very long and complicated part of your overall accident investigation. The more time spent drawing and practicing this skill, the easier it will become the following time.

THIS PAGE INTENTIONALLY LEFT BLANK

10

BASIC SKID ANALYSIS

INTRODUCTION

Traffic collision analysis can be made easier by the use of physical evidence which remains at the scene. Evidence such as skidmarks can become a valuable clue as to how the collision occurred. Many of us have seen skidmarks at a collision scene but never really gave them a second thought. To the public, a skidmark may simply mean a vehicle was involved in a traffic accident. The trained traffic accident investigator will draw several different conclusions from these same marks. The skidmarks remaining at the scene may be considered crucial to establishing a vehicle's speed and direction of travel prior to and after the impact. These marks will also provide the investigator with the vehicle's potential braking efficiency that will lead to a estimate of the speed prior to impact.

This chapter will focus on interpretation of the skidmark as evidence and the role it plays in the officer's conclusions of how the accident took place. In this chapter you will be introduced to several basic skid analysis formulas, which once solved, can yield a minimum vehicle speed. Each of the formulas discussed in this chapter will have a specific application in accident investigation. The formulas and principals found in the following pages are not unique only to the accident investigation community, but can be found in several physics and engineering manuals. This area of accident investigation is not meant to confuse the investigator but to contribute to the overall scope of the investigation. The officer simply needs a basic grasp of algebraic skills to solve these equations. We will be discussing the application of these formulas in the following pages.

WHAT IS A SKIDMARK?

A *skidmark* can be described as a mark left upon any surface by a wheel either locked or rotating. The term *"skidmark"* includes all evidence of skidding such as scuffing even if no rubber from the tire is left behind. We have all observed these skidmarks during the course of our travels over city streets and highways. Each of these marks may be the result of accidents, but others may be the result of different influences placed upon the vehicle. Skidmarks can be affected by several factors. These may include outside influences such as roadway conditions, weather, and vehicle braking efficiency.

There are *three* basic methods of leaving visible skidmarks:

1. ***Extreme Deceleration*:** The braking system of the vehicle causes the wheel to cease rotating.

2. ***Extreme Change of Direction*:** This may result from an intentional effort on the part of the driver or an impact/contact with a vehicle or other fixed object.

3. ***Extreme Acceleration*:** Occurs when a propelling force or thrust is generated in an amount exceeding the pavement efficiency.

SKIDMARK CLASSIFICATION

Skidmarks can be divided into nine major categories. These categories have been created to classify a skidmark. Once the marks have been categorized, they can be analyzed based on their importance in the overall investigation.

1. ***Impending*:** Wheel rotating slower than the forward motion of the vehicle.

2. ***Locked Wheel Skid*:** Non-rotating wheel moving in a straight or curved line in the original direction of travel.

3. ***Side Skid*:** A locked, braked, or rotating wheel of a vehicle sliding in other than a forward direction, except when known to be caused by a centrifugal force.

4. ***Critical Speed Scuff*:** Rotating wheel of a vehicle rounding a curve or turning at such a speed that centrifugal force entirely or partially overcomes the frictional resistance of the surface it is riding on.

5. ***Skip Skid*:** Left by a locked wheel that bounces off the surface it is riding on.

6. ***Gap Skid*:** Left by a locked-wheel that is released then locked again.

7. ***Acceleration Skid*:** Propelling force or thrust generated by the tires in an amount exceeding the pavement efficiency.

8. ***Collision Scrub:***	A short, broad skidmark made during the engagement of the vehicles in a collision.
9. ***Tire Mark:***	The impression, prints, or rolling marks left upon a roadway or other surface.

Besides these *nine* categories, skids may also manifest themselves in various forms and shapes. These physical influences may be in the form of side impact, shifting loads and rotating vehicle center of mass. For these reasons, skidmarks may take on several different appearances.

SKIDMARK DOCUMENTATION

Each skidmark must be measured and documented if it is to be used in your accident investigation conclusion. The same techniques may be utilized in this measurement process. The length of a skidmark will have an effect on your speed analysis calculations if the information is not gathered properly. For this reason alone, take care and pay attention to detail when collecting this information. Remember to *walk* your collision scene and make a mental note of the skidmarks you wish to document.

Skidmarks do not need to be marked and painted as in a fatal accident scene unless you are choosing to measure them in a *reference line* and *reference point* method. Check your departmental policies for direction on which scenes you will need to reproduce in this manner. Marking a skidmark regardless of the severity of the accident may assist you in visualizing the direction the involved vehicles traveled. This marking may simply consist of a horseshoe mark at the beginning and end of the skidmark similar to what was discussed in chapter 9 (Diagramming).

Skidmark

Marking a skid in this manner will give the accident investigator a view of the evidence from many different angles. The officer will not lose the true overall measurement length due to changing roadway or lighting conditions. This will also not leave a permanent mark on the roadway. Getting down or slightly above the mark may give a perspective of the mark that was not visible from an earlier vantage point.

Several methods of measuring the skidmark are acceptable. The following will be a list of the most commonly used tools in skidmark analysis.

1. ***Pacing:*** This method tends to be the most inaccurate. Each officer's stride cannot be accounted for in the calculation phase of the speed analysis.

2. ***Roll-a-tape:*** This tool is *good* for long distances, but many officers fail to check the accuracy of the device on a regular basis. Officers may also fail to walk in a straight line while measuring a mark and therefore collect a possible inflated estimate.

3. ***Tape measures:*** Steel, plastic, cloth and fiberglass tape measuring tools have proven to be the most accurate. Unintentional errors by the operators can be avoided.

LONGEST SKID VS. AVERAGE SKID

Each skid on the roadway should be examined and categorized according to the earlier discussed techniques. Many vehicles leave only one mark or a portion of the skidmark behind on the roadway surface. How then can this be helpful to the investigator? Skidmark analysis will yield the highest potential *minimum vehicle speed.* For this reason, we must decide to either measure the *longest* of the remaining skids or average *all* of the skids.

The most accurate of these would be to average the remaining skidmarks. The rule of thumb for me is to be as *fair* as possible and give the *benefit of doubt* to the parties involved. This will give you credibility in the area of accident investigation. Remember the evidence *speaks for itself.* This means any investigator should be able to examine your work and agree you have not been prejudicial to their client. This should be a benchmark for you, and should not cause you to either under-estimate or over-estimate the length of the mark. Obvious *under-braking* or *over-braking* will somewhat contaminate your average when you are trying to be fair. If this is the case, you may wish to choose two instead of three marks for you're *longest vs. average length.*

BRAKING EFFICIENCY

Each rotating wheel on a vehicle *brakes* at a different rate. This may be due largely in part to tire wear, brake pad wear, weight placement, and other factors. An estimate of the vehicle's braking efficiency by the investigating officer will be necessary. The braking efficiency in a vehicle can largely influence how fast the vehicle could have been traveling. The higher the braking efficiency, the higher the potential accompanying vehicle speed will be. The chart below is based on potential braking efficiency estimates on both front wheel and rear wheel drive vehicles. The difference noted in the two is the result of the increased weight of the drive axle mounted at the front of the vehicle.

Braking Efficiency

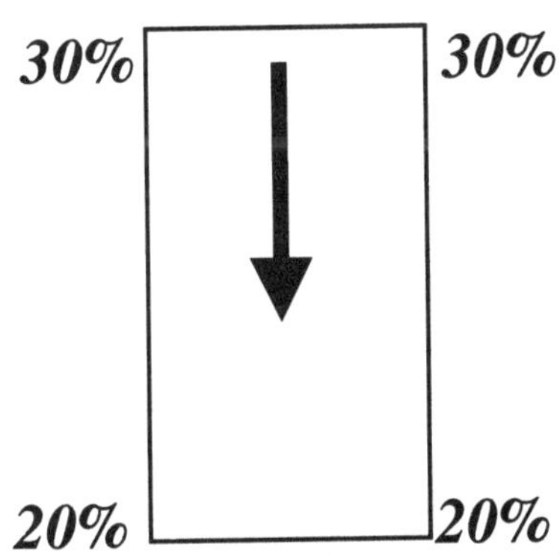

Rear wheel drive

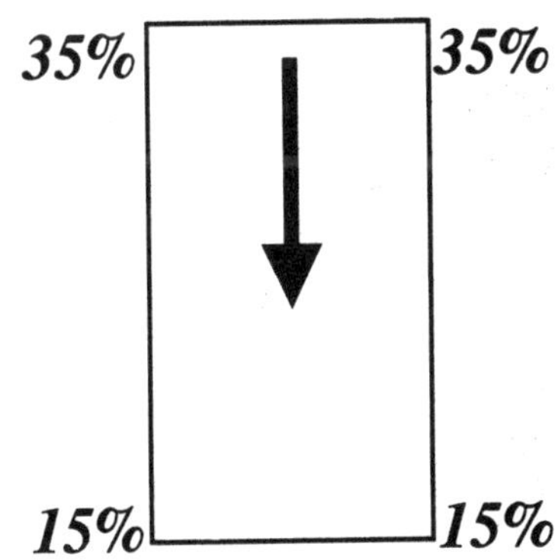

Front wheel drive

The investigating officer will need to estimate the overall braking efficiency of the vehicle that is being inspected. This estimate will be later added to the formula used in calculating the vehicle's *minimum* highest potential speed. Utilize impending skids in both your length measurements and braking efficiency estimates. The skidmarks that remain on the roadway tend to provide you with the best potential braking estimate.

DRAG FACTOR AND COEFFICIENT OF FRICTION

Each of the above terms means essentially the same in the accident investigator's vocabulary. The term *coefficient of friction* is being utilized more often in the accident investigation world. The true definition of the two will be the same. Drag factor or coefficient of friction is a *measurement of the resistance of an object sliding over a known surface*. This could include but not be limited to asphalt, cement, grass, dirt, etc.

Many years ago, this factor was calculated using a *drag sled*. The drag sled was a known weight and was pulled over a known surface. A scale in foot pounds was used to calculate the force needed to move a drag sled over the selected surface. These figures were then placed into a mathematical formula to calculate the drag factor/coefficient of friction.

DRAG SLED

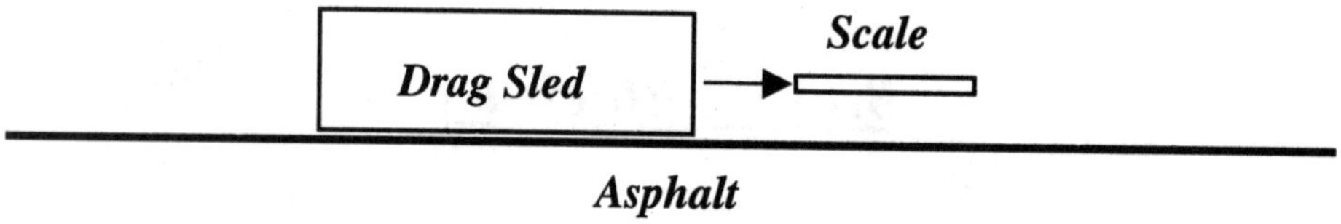

DRAG FACTOR/COEFFICIENT OF FRICTION FORMULA

The drag factor/coefficient of friction can be calculated if the proper information is known. The formula below will provide the investigator with the drag factor or coefficient of friction.

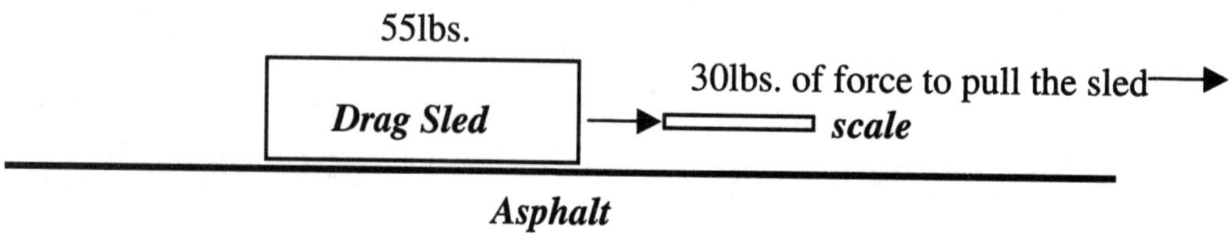

Drag Factor Formula:

F = Force
***W* = Weight**

$$f = \frac{F}{W}$$

The weight of the sled was measured at *55 lb.* The force needed to move the sled was measured at *30 lb.* These measurements can then be placed into the formula above. Solving the formula will give us a coefficient of friction or drag factor. Let's test the formula and solve for the drag factor.

$$f = \frac{30\text{lbs.}}{55\text{lbs.}} = .54$$

Most investigators no longer use drag sleds with the development of today's modern drag factor computer technology. Charts are also available in many accident manuals that have tested several surfaces and have completed the math for you. These charts are printed and can be used as a quick reference guide when trying to gain a rough estimate of a vehicle's speed. The charts give a general possible high and low drag factor estimate for the listed roadway. A more accurate way of measuring the drag factor is to test the roadway utilizing a second investigator. This can be accomplished utilizing a radar gun, a two-way radio, and a vehicle.

The investigator should choose a vehicle similar to the one involved in the collision. This is not a mandatory part of the equipment; however, a similar vehicle will give you more accurate information. Another officer will drive the test vehicle and lay a series of skids over the area where the collision occurred. The officer will leave *three* test skids at a known speed. This will provide the investigator with *three skids* and *three speeds*. These will then be averaged and placed into a formula that will yield a drag factor.

The investigating officer will position himself at a safe area to the side of the collision scene. He will instruct his partner to drive the test vehicle in the direction of where the collision took place. The investigating officer will utilize the radar gun to gain a consistent speed on the approaching test vehicle. Once the vehicle reaches the desired speed, the officer will direct the driver of the vehicle to *"slam on the vehicle's brakes."* This test will be repeated *three* times. Depending on the approximate speeds, the following results could potentially be obtained using this method. A target speed of 45 mph was used in the scenario depicted below.

Test Skids:

1. ***100 feet @ 45 mph***
2. ***110 feet @ 46 mph***
3. ***99 feet @ 44 mph***

These skids and speeds will be averaged providing the investigating officer with a skid length of *103 feet* and an average speed of *45 mph.* After averaging the skid lengths and speeds, the information is placed into a formula which yields a drag factor/coefficient of friction value.

Drag factor formula:

S = speed in miles per hour
d = distance in feet
f = friction

$$f = \frac{S^2}{30d}$$

The average speed of the test was *45 mph.* The average skid test length was found to be *103 feet.* These values are then placed in the previous formula and the equation is solved. The *45 mph* speed is substituted for the "S" and *103 feet* is substituted for "d". The constant is "30" in the equation and does not change.

Speed = 45 mph
Distance = 103 feet

$$f = \frac{(45\ mph)^2}{(30)(103)}$$

$$f = \frac{(2025)}{(3090)}$$

$$f = .65$$

Portable computers similar in size to a unit mounted radar system have since replaced the older drag sled measurement. These systems provide the investigator with a drag factor/coefficient of friction measurement accurate to the thousandth decimal place. These tools have made the calculation phase of this formula obsolete. The computer is placed into the test vehicle and a several skids are placed on the roadway where the collision took place. The computer is removed from the test vehicle and examined. The computer will provide the investigating officer with several facts concerning the vehicle used in the test. The computer calculates the highest, lowest, and average drag factor/coefficient of friction during the entire skid. The portable computer is downloaded into a main line computer. The charts and graphs of the information obtained during the test skids are available and can be printed and attached to your investigative reports.

Drag Factor / Coefficient of Friction Chart

Description of Roadway Surface	*Dry* *Less than 30 mph*	*Dry* *More than 30 mph*	*Wet* *Less than 30 mph*	*Wet* *More than 30 mph*
1. Concrete				
New & Sharp	*.80 - 1.00*	*.70 - .85*	*.50 - .80*	*.40 - .75*
Traveled	*.60 - .80*	*.60 - .80*	*.45 - .70*	*.45 - .65*
Traffic polished	*.55 - .75*	*.50 - .65*	*.45 - .65*	*.45 - .60*
2. Asphalt or Tar				
New & Sharp	*.80 - 1.00*	*.65 - .70*	*.50 - .80*	*.45 - .75*
Traveled	*.60 - .80*	*.40 - .70*	*.45 -.70*	*.40 - .65*
3. Gravel				
Packed, oiled	*.55 - .85*	*.50 - .80*	*.40 - .80*	*.40 - .60*
Loose	*.40 - .70*	*.40 - .70*	*.45 - .75*	*.45 - .75*
4. Ice				
Smooth	*.10 - .25*	*.07 - .20*	*.05 - .10*	*.05 - .10*
5. Snow				
Packed	*.30 - .55*	*.35 - .55*	*.30 - .60*	*.30 - .60*

The Drag Factor/Coefficient of Friction Chart reflects the frictional values for the many roadway surfaces you may encounter. Use the average of the high and low frictional values, e.g. dry traveled asphalt roadway more than 30 mph (.40 - .70 = .55), but the ultimate decision is up to the investigator as to which drag factor/coefficient of friction numeric value to use. The values listed are provided in such a manner as to facilitate frictional value averaging. The differences in these values reflect roadway, vehicle, and weight factors. For this reason, it is recommended that you average the value rather than relying directly on what is printed. Either method is acceptable. For obvious reasons, the majority of accident investigators prefer to use a factor pictured in the chart. Experiment with calculating a coefficient of friction factor utilizing test skids to fully understand how the principle works.

SPEED & VELOCITY

Before we can truly understand how a vehicle skids to a stop, we must examine the different forms of measurement. A vehicle moves down the roadway in what most of us assume is a measured speed. A *"speedometer"* has been placed into the dash of the vehicle to help us calculate this speed. The majority of our nation's highways have a speed limit posted on it. *"Speed"* is traditionally measured in *miles per hour.* This is reflected on the face of the speedometer. Therefore we tend to consistently think in this form of expression. A vehicle's speed however may also be measured in a very short length of time over the distance of a skidmark. For this reason we must also be able to calculate the movement of a vehicle in a much more accurate sense. Rather than only manipulating a vehicle's speed in *miles per hour,* we may express the movement in *feet per second.* The following definitions of this movement define the main difference.

Velocity: Velocity is the measurement of the distance traveled in a known period of time. This measurement is expressed in *feet per second* or *fps.*

Speed: Speed can also be a measurement of time and distance, but it is expressed in *miles per hour* or *mph.*

Since the majority of us express vehicle movement in *miles per hour,* how can this be converted into *feet per second?* A formula has been created that will accomplish the conversion in a fast and simple manner.

	What do I have?	What do I want to know?
1.	***Miles per hour (speed = S)***	***Feet per second (Velocity = V)***
	Miles per hour x 1.467	***equals the measurement in fps***
	What do I have?	**What do I want to know?**
2.	***Feet per second (Velocity = V)***	***Miles per hour (Speed = S)***
	Feet per second x .6818	***equals the measurement in mph***

Let's test the *mph (miles per hour)* to *fps (feet per second)* formula...

60 mph converted to fps

60 mph x 1.467 = 88.02 fps

therefore ***V or Velocity = 88.02 fps***

For reference, we will be using the letter "*S*" when expressing an answer or formula in *miles per hour.* The letter "*V*" will be used when expressing the formula or answer in *feet per second.* This will simplify the thought process when the information is calculated using a specific formula.

Let's try converting *fps (feet per second)* to *mph (miles per hour).*

88.02 fps converted to mph

88.02 fps x .6818 = 60.01 mph

therefore ***S or Speed = 60 mph***

Many times formulas will have the conversion factors built in to simplify the calculation phase of the process. We will be examining a select few of these formulas in this introduction to skid analysis. The provided formulas will give you a basic understanding of how *Speed (S) in miles per hour* and *Velocity (V) in feet per second* will play a major role in assisting you in to understand just what occurred in various phases of the accident. The first of these formulas will clearly demonstrate the need to convert *miles per hour* into *feet per second.*

KNOWN SPEED & TIME

Earlier we explained the measurement of a vehicle's movement and the manner in which the majority of Americans understand it. The general public refers to traveling time in a measurement of an hour. This is compounded by the way a vehicle speedometer itself is marked and calibrated. The face of the speedometer is usually marked in increments of *5 mph.* A vehicle accident, however, takes place in a matter of seconds. For this reason, the accident investigator must use a much more precise measurement.

If a vehicle is traveling at a known speed in *mph*, we can calculate how far in *feet* the same vehicle traveled in a known matter of time *(t)*. The speed *(S)* of the vehicle is expressed currently in *mph* and will need to be converted into *fps* before this can be accomplished. The following formula will be used to provide us with this answer.

Time/Distance formula:

$$d = Vt$$

What I want to know	What I have
Distance (d) in feet	***Speed (S) in mph*** ***Time (t) in Seconds***

Let's test the formula using *35 mph* as the speed *(S)* and *5 seconds* as the time *(t).*

First the speed *(S)* of the vehicle must be converted into *fps* from *mph.*

35 mph x 1.467 = 51.345 fps

The Velocity (V) = 51.345 fps

Now that the Speed *(S)* of the vehicle has been converted, we can place the known numbers in the formula.

Time/Distance Formula:

$$d = Vt$$

The distance *(d) = unknown*	*d = (51.345 fps)(5 seconds)*
The velocity *(V) = 51.345 fps*	
The time *(t) = 5 seconds*	*d = 256.725 feet* **rounded up to** *256.73*

A simple reminder: this measurement is in *tenths* not *twelfths* and must be converted before it can be accurately reflected using a steel tape.

SLIDE TO STOP

A vehicle traveling on the roadway leaves trace evidence on the street each time the vehicle is accelerated or decelerated rapidly. This evidence can provide the investigator with a clue such as how fast the vehicle was potentially traveling before the brakes were applied. Factors such as braking efficiency, roadway type, and vehicle weight may also play a factor in this calculation process. Once the drag factor or coefficient of friction of the roadway and braking efficiency has been determined or estimated, the next phase of the calculation can begin.

Two formulas have been developed for the investigator to use in this scenario. The first formula will yield the answer in *miles per hour.* The second formula is slightly more complicated, but provides the answer in *feet per second.* Once the answer is obtained, a conversion formula may be used to place the answer in the appropriate form of measurement. The preferred way is to choose a formula which has the *conversion factor* built into it that does not require a secondary calculation after the answer has been obtained.

Slide to Stop formula in *mph:*

$$S = \sqrt{30(d)(f)(e)}$$

What I want to know	**What I have**
Speed (S) in mph	*Distance (d)* *Friction (f)* *braking efficiency (e)* *30 is a constant*

Clue: The formula provides the answer in *mph* and therefore no conversion is necessary.

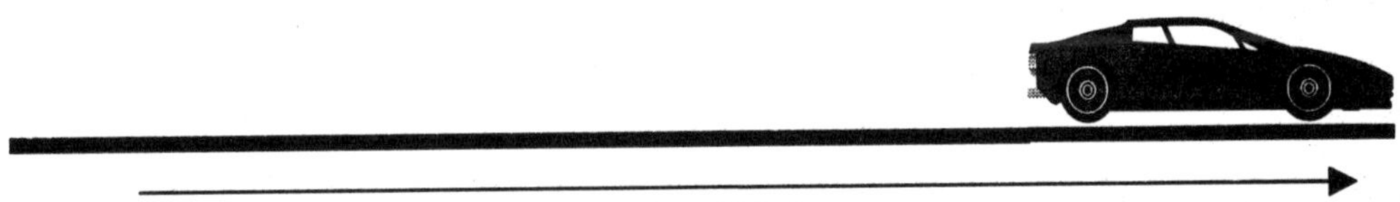

d = 100 feet
Traveled asphalt roadway

CHOOSING THE RIGHT BRAKING EFFICIENCY

In the scenario on the previous page, the vehicle slid to a stop on a *"traveled asphalt"* roadway. For the purpose of this example, the vehicle left a skid length of *100 feet.* Braking efficiency and the role it plays in calculating the speed of the vehicle was mentioned earlier. Very few vehicles will display *100%* of their breaking efficiency. In this case, we will use *100%* to simplify the mathematical portion of the equation. Because we are using *100% braking*, we do not need to place this into the formula. *100%* equals *1.0* once converted into tenths for the equation and will not affect the answer. 1.0 multiplied by a number does not change the number. The converted percentage in this equation has been left to help you visualize how the formula works.

CHOOSING THE RIGHT DRAG OR COEFFICIENT OF FRICTION FACTOR

.55 has been selected as the drag factor coefficient from the table on the previous pages. Checking the table for *"dry traveled asphalt"* above *30 mph,* I averaged the drag factors *.4 and .7* and arrived at this factor. You may however wish to use both a *.4 and .7* and run the formula separately which will yield a *high* and *low* possible *minimum speed.* After using this formula for awhile you will start to become familiar with which skids should be calculated at *"more than 30 mph"* vs. *"less than 30 mph"* on the chart.

Slide to Stop Formula in *mph:*

$$Speed\ (S) = \sqrt{30(d)(f)(e)}$$

Distance = 100 feet
Drag factor = .55

$$Speed\ (S) = \sqrt{30(100)(.55)(1.0)}$$

Braking = 100 % or 1.0

$$Speed\ (S) = \sqrt{1650}$$

$$Speed\ (S) = 40.6201\ mph\ or\ 41\ mph$$

Slide to Stop in *fps:*

The second formula will provide the investigator with the answer in *feet per second* rather than in *mph*. The purpose of learning both formulas will become important in later phases of accident investigation. Many accident investigators work all of their respective calculations in *fps* and convert the answer into *mph* after the formula has been solved. Others work through all of the formulas strictly in *mph* and convert the answer into *fps* when needed. The investigator must be proficient in both formulas for those cases where he or she faces an accident investigator in court with this ability.

Slide to Stop in *fps:*

$$V = \sqrt{2(a)(d)}$$

What I want to know	What I have
Velocity (V) in fps	*Acceleration (a)* *Distance (d)* *2 is a constant*

From solving the previous formula, you will recognize the symbol *"d"* which is the distance of the skid. *Acceleration (a)* is a new symbol in this formula. Acceleration can either be positive or negative depending on the force being applied to the wheels at the moment it is measured. For the purposes of this book we will not discuss how this is obtained, but what can be substituted for it to solve the above equation.

Acceleration:

$$a = (g)(f)$$

Gravity *(g)* is a constant at *32.2 fps*^{2}
Friction *(f)* is the determined drag factor

The previous series of symbols can be substituted in the *slide to stop formula (fps)*. The formula can be solved with this additional information as follows. Using the same skid length and drag factor from the previous page, we will solve the equation that yields the answer in *fps* rather than *mph*.

Distance(d) = 100 feet
Acceleration (a) = (g)(f)
Friction (f) = .55 from the chart for "dry traveled asphalt"
Gravity (g) = 32.2 fps^2
Braking efficiency (e) = 100% or 1.0

Slide to Stop in *fps:*

$$\text{Velocity } (V) = \sqrt{2(a)(d)(e)}$$

$$\text{Velocity } (V) = \sqrt{2(g)(f)(d)(e)}$$

We have substituted *Gravity (g) &*
Friction (f) for Acceleration (a)

$$\text{Velocity } (V) = \sqrt{2(32.2)(.55)(100)(1.0)}$$

$$\text{Velocity } (V) = \sqrt{3542}$$

$$\text{Velocity } (V) = 59.5147 \text{ fps or } 59.51 \text{ fps}$$

DISTANCE TO STOP

Each day we witness drivers following vehicles directly in front of them. The people behind the wheel of these vehicles believe they can stop at a moment's notice. This of course is unreasonable due to the human factor of *reaction time*. Reaction time comes into play in almost every accident scenario. The time needed to perceive a hazard and respond to it can quickly diminish the safety buffer between two vehicles. The majority of rear-end traffic collisions result not only from following too closely at an unsafe speed, but from the additional reaction time needed to perceive and react to the hazard itself.

Reaction time can be affected by many things; *e.g.* alcohol, drugs, distracting conversation, or other outside interference. The standard reaction time in the accident investigation industry has been estimated to be approximately *1.5 seconds*. This measurement of time seems fast, but a traffic collision occurs much faster. A single skid in a traffic collision may only last for a second or two before impact. The higher the speed, the longer the distance the vehicle will travel before the braking system is applied. You may be called upon to calculate a possible stopping distance for a vehicle that is traveling at a known speed on a given surface.

Distance to Stop formula in *feet*:

$$d = \frac{S^2}{30f}$$

What I want to know	What I have
Distance (d) in feet	*Speed (S) in mph* *Friction (f)*

Traveled asphalt roadway @ 35 mph

Distance (d) = unknown
Speed (S) = 35 mph
friction (f) = .55

$$d = \frac{S^2}{30f}$$

$$d = \frac{35^2}{30(.55)}$$

$$d = \frac{1225}{16.5}$$

d = 74.24 feet or 74 feet and 3 inches

The answer listed above will be the minimum distance a vehicle will need in order to completely stop once the driver realizes he or she needs to panic-stop. This distance does not reflect any additional reaction time. The vehicle would travel a much further distance before the driver can panic stop as stated above when reaction time has been added. Once this has been completed, these two distances can be combined for a total stopping estimate. To calculate this additional distance, we must convert the known speed from *mph* into *fps*. Once this is accomplished, we may apply the *time distance* formula discussed in the previous pages.

$$d = (V)t$$

For this example, we know the vehicle was traveling at a rate of *35 mph* prior to the *panic braking*. The speed of the vehicle must be converted and placed in the formula.

The clue in the formula is *Velocity*. To place the speed of the vehicle in this formula, we must multiply it by the conversion factor of *1.467*, which will yield the speed in a *Velocity style measurement of fps*.

Distance (d) = unknown
Speed (S) = 35 mph
Velocity (V) = 35 mph x 1.467
Perception/Reaction time (t) = 1.5 seconds

To convert *mph* to *fps*, we must multiply the initial speed as indicated above.

35 mph x 1.467 = 51.345 fps

This converted measurement can then be placed in the *Time/Distance* formula along with the estimated *perception/reaction time* of *1.5 seconds*.

d = V(t)
d = (51.345)(1.5)
d = 77.0175 feet

The above answer reflects the distance the vehicle traveled at *35 mph* while the driver perceived and reacted to the hazard before applying the brakes. This measurement will be added to the previous answer (distance to stop of 74.24 feet) when explaining the *total safe stopping distance.* To sum this all up, refer to the following diagram.

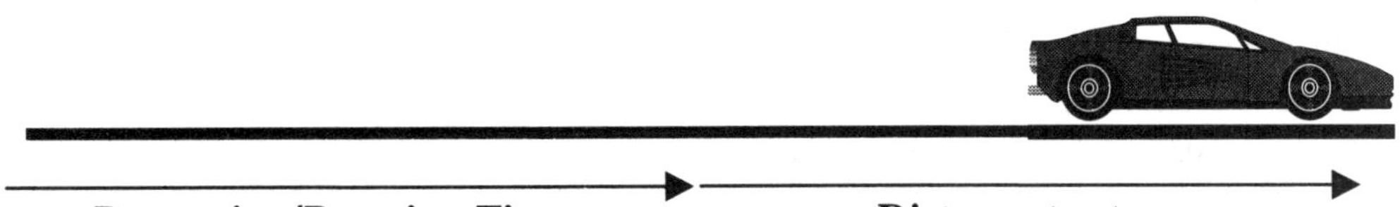

From the example above, you can see the distance to stop the vehicle is close to the distance traveled during the *perception/reaction time* portion of this collision.

REAR END COLLISIONS

The demonstration above depicts a vehicle trying to stop to avoid a hazard. The vehicle following the one attempting to stop also must perceive the hazard (vehicle stopping in front of him) and react to this. The distance the secondary vehicle travels is the vehicle's speed in *fps* multiplied by the *perception/reaction time* of *1.5 seconds.* This added travel distance due to the driver's *perception/reaction time* are what cause a *rear end collision.* The main difference is the front vehicle may actually avoid the hazard and stop safely. The secondary vehicle is following too closely at an *unsafe speed* and cannot avoid the stopping vehicle.

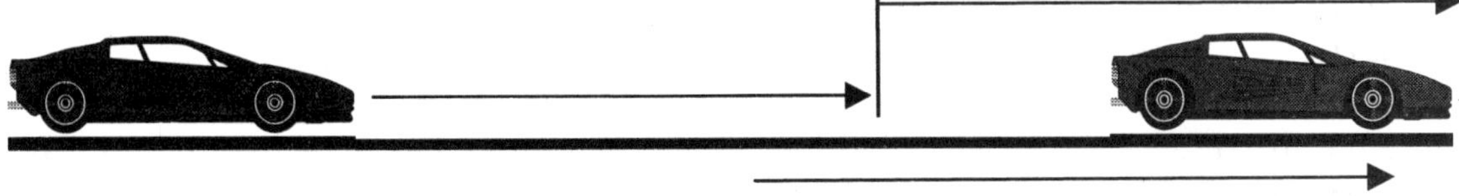

The example above depicts vehicle #1 (on the left) following vehicle #2 (on the right) at *35 mph.* Vehicle number #2 suddenly applies the brakes and panic stops. The driver in vehicle #1 will travel a distance of *77.0175 feet* before he perceives the hazard of vehicle #2 stopping. Vehicle #2 slides to a stop in a distance of approximately *77.24 feet.* Vehicle #1 then travels the entire stopping distance of vehicle #2 @ *74.24 feet* while still perceiving the hazard of vehicle #2 stopping. Driver #1 must then travel an additional distance of *74.24 feet* himself before stopping. This of course is not possible and vehicle #1 strikes the rear of vehicle #2, absorbing the additional distance. Vehicle #1 should have a safety buffer of approximately 77.0175 feet while following Vehicle #2 to avoid this collision. This estimate does not include the additional measurement of the axle to the front bumper of Vehicle #1.

In reality, most drivers do not allow themselves this extra stopping distance. They rely on instinct instead of a safety buffer. Most drivers brake slowly as they perceive hazards on the roadway allowing a much further distance for the drivers following them to react. This does however explain those multiple vehicle accidents on the interstate highways. The vehicle at the front of the pack may actually have avoided the initial hazard, but is rear ended by several vehicles who were following too close to avoid the hazard themselves. These vehicles then collide with the rear of the stopped vehicle that originally avoided the hazard at hand.

Many of you are probably asking why do we not find the driver at fault with a primary collision factor of *"following too closely"* rather than *"unsafe speed."* The vehicle code in part states each driver on the roadway must maintain control of his/her vehicle at all times and be able to avoid hazards present. The vehicle code section for *"following too closely"* is more of an observed violation before a collision occurs. You may use the example above to substantiate a violation of this section in a court appearance. The formula is based on both vehicles utilizing *100%* of their braking efficiency.

SPEED FROM RADIUS

A vehicle's approximate speed can be gathered from a *"yawing"* skidmark while traversing a curve of the roadway. These *"yaw marks"* have often times been referred to as *"centrifugal skidmarks"* as well. Either of these references is acceptable for the purposes of accident investigation and skid analysis. The outstanding quality of these marks is that they will give the accident investigator an insight into the speed of the vehicle with very little contamination. The vehicle in essence leaves a *"impending"* mark upon the roadway as it struggles to maintain a grip of the roadway surface. A mathematical formula has been developed to assist the accident investigator in solving this puzzle.

Before the speed *(S)* of the vehicle can be determined, we must calculate the *radius* of the *yaw* or *centrifugal skidmark.* This can be accomplished in the same manner as the radius of a curve was determined in the diagramming chapter of this book. The formula is essentially the same; only the *middle ordinate* and *chord* measurements can potentially be much larger.

<u>Radius of a curve:</u>

$$R = \frac{C^2}{8m} \quad \frac{m}{2}$$

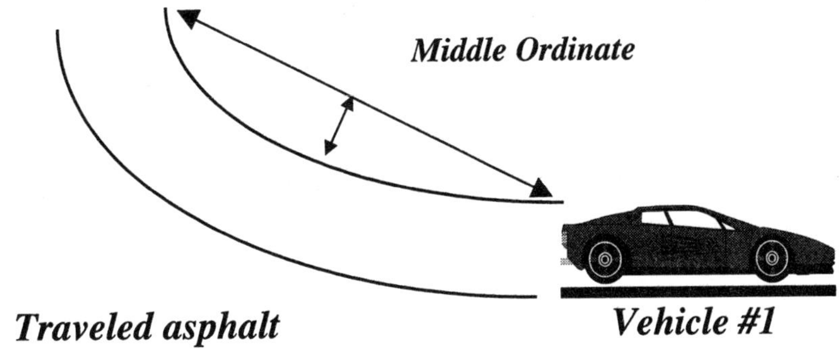

For this example equation, we will use the following measurements to solve the formula on the previous page.

Chord = 80 feet
Middle ordinate = 5 feet Reminder - The middle ordinate is taken at a 90 degree angle and is placed at the ½ way point on the chord.

Clue - *The measurements should be taken as early in the curve as possible to yield a higher critical speed.*

Radius Formula:

$$r = \frac{C^2}{8m} \quad \frac{m}{2}$$

$$r = \frac{(80')^2}{8(5')} \quad \frac{(5')}{2}$$

$$r = \frac{(6400')}{(40')} \quad \frac{(5')}{2}$$

$$r = 160 + 2.5$$

$$r = 162.5 \text{ feet}$$

Once this equation has been solved, the answer reached will be placed into a secondary formula. This formula, once solved, will provide us with the approximate *minimum speed* of the vehicle as the skid occurred on the roadway.

CRITICAL SPEED FROM YAW MARKS

The objective of this formula will be to determine a critical speed from loss of stability in a curve. This loss in speed is directly proportional to the force applied to the vehicle. The radius of the yaw mark has been determined from the previous example as *162.5 feet.* The following formula will provide us with the speed of the vehicle in *mph* rather than *fps*.

Critical Speed From Yaw Marks:

$$\text{Speed (S)} = 3.86\sqrt{r(f \pm e)}$$

What I want to know	What I have
Speed (S) in mph	*Radius (r) in feet* *Friction (f)* *Elevation (e) %* *Constant 3.86*

Speed from radius formula:

Speed (S) = unknown
Radius (r) = 162.5
Elevation (e) = Level in this case
Friction (f) = .55 averaged traveled asphalt value from the chart
Constant = 3.86

$$\text{Speed (S)} = 3.86\sqrt{r(f \pm e)}$$

$$\text{Speed (S)} = 3.86\sqrt{162.5(.55 \pm 0.0)}$$

$$\text{Speed (S)} = 3.86\sqrt{162.5(.55)}$$

$$\text{Speed (S)} = 3.86\sqrt{89.375}$$

$$\text{Speed (S)} = (3.86)(9.453)$$

$$\text{Speed (S)} = 36.491 \text{ mph or } 36 \text{ mph}$$

Many times a yaw mark will be left upon a roadway that rises or descends. The frictional value of the roadway must reflect this change in grade. For this reason, a portion of the formula allows for a rise or lowering of the frictional value. The previous example reflects a flat level surface and therefore a change in the value was not necessary. Let's try to solve the speed from radius formula in which a rise in the yaw mark leaves the roadway. For the purposes of this example, you are provided with the appropriate radius value and change in grade.

Speed (S) = unknown
Radius (r) = 314.5
Friction (f) = .70 averaged for a traveled concrete surface
Elevation (e) = 4 % rise in grade or .04
Constant = 3.86

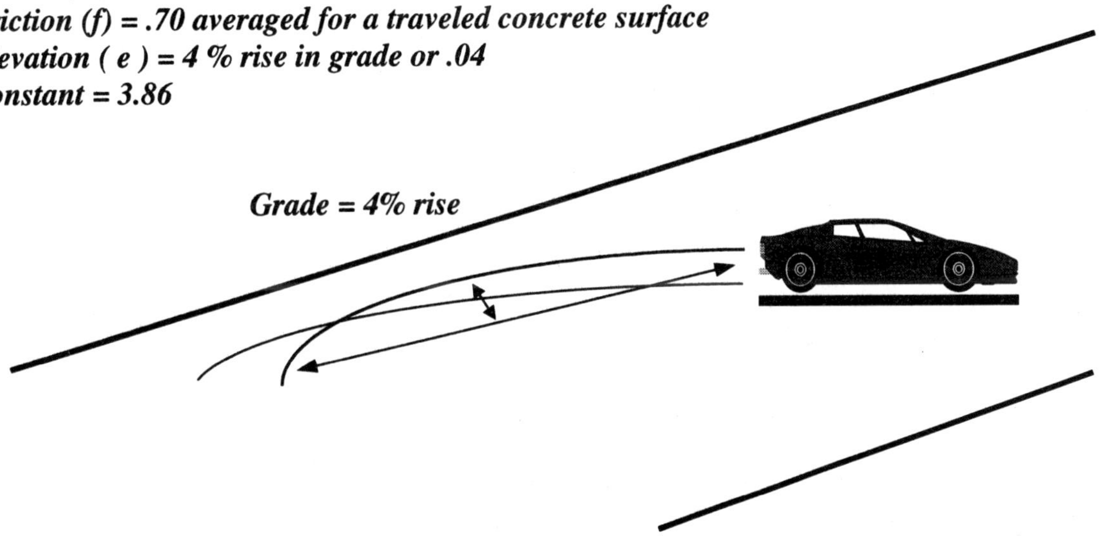

Solving speed from radius with a grade:

$$Speed\ (S) = 3.86\sqrt{r(f \pm e)}$$

$$Speed\ (S) = 3.86\sqrt{314.5(.70 \pm .04)}$$

$$Speed\ (S) = 3.86\sqrt{314.5(.74)}$$

$$Speed\ (S) = 3.86\sqrt{232.73}$$

$$Speed\ (S) = (3.86)(15.225)$$

$$Speed\ (S) = 58.886 \text{ mph or } 59 \text{ mph}$$

The high radius value should not confuse you in the radius calculation phase. Depending on the potential speed, the radius could be extremely high. Once this is placed into the speed from radius formula, the higher number will be factored out. The example above depicts a centrifugal skidmark that rose on a banked roadway. A vehicle that slides down in the skid will have the percentage of grade subtracted from the frictional value.

WHEN DOES IT END?

The formulas and equations on the previous pages are meant to give you a basic understanding of how skid analysis plays a role in accident investigation. Each of these formulas, if used properly, will provide you with an additional tool in making the final determination of *how the collision may have occurred.* Those of you who chose to continue forward in your accident investigation training will see these and many more formulas. Choosing the right formula for the evidence present will become easier as time goes on. It is suggested that you use these formulas as often as possible to become more familiar with them. Many officers write the formulas on a cheat sheet in the folder of their respective calculator's cases for quick reference, or you may contact LawTech (see back cover) for information about how to obtain a field reference manual version of this book, which contains the formulas.

These formulas of course are designed for ideal situations where no other contaminating factors are present. This means that the vehicle strikes a pedestrian or bicycle, both of which have a *negligible effect* on the striking vehicle's speed. A vehicle that collides with a solid object such as a tree, building, or other vehicle may have continued in the same direction if the outside force had not acted upon it. Essentially, *Newton's law of motion* states a body in motion will continue in motion until an outside force acts upon it. This force could be in the form of a frictional value or a secondary striking vehicle.

Many of the formulas necessary to solve these problems will be discussed in the more advanced classes of accident investigation. You are encouraged to check your answers with someone who is well versed in math or accident reconstruction. A translated number, or key-stroke error on your calculator, may have a devastating effect on the party being found at fault in the collision. The key to accurate accident investigation analysis is *taking your time and doing it right the first time.*

11

HIT AND RUN

WHAT MAKES PEOPLE RUN?

Many of the traffic collisions we investigate result in an added charge of *hit and run* simply because one or more of the involved parties refuses to remain at the scene. California, like many other states, has laws against fleeing the scene of an accident. The charge of *hit and run* may be enhanced due to the injuries of the parties who remained at the scene. But the question still remains: *why leave the scene of a collision?"* A collision is not a crime and the drivers cannot be arrested unless another chargeable crime arises out of the accident investigation itself. Many of the parties involved in traffic collisions may not want to accept financial responsibility for their actions. Others may have more motivating factors for not remaining at the scene. These might include their driver's license status, outstanding warrants, or being involved in a crime at the time the collision first occurred. For whatever reason they flee the scene, it is the investigating officer's responsibility to solve this puzzle.

A collision scene is not unlike any other crime scene. Evidence, witnesses, and clues to the identity of the suspect may all remain at the scene. The right investigator can piece together many of the unknown aspects of the accident. The suspect vehicle itself may have left clues that tell you what occurred prior to the collision. Pieces of the suspect vehicle and other evidence may have been knocked off the vehicle before it fled the scene. These can then later be matched to a possible vehicle for identification. Solving a hit and run accident can be challenging, but not impossible for the investigating officer. The right approach combined with a working knowledge of the subject can yield excellent results.

MINIMAL INFORMATION

You have made contact with a very distraught victim of a traffic collision. The driver stated he was struck by a mid size Chevy Impala 2 door, light blue in color. The driver of the collision even provides you with a possible license plate of the suspect vehicle. This information sounds great and will provide the investigating officer with a starting point.

What the citizen does not realize is he or she may not be able to identify the driver. Most citizens look carefully at the suspect vehicle as it leaves the scene and truly believe a license plate number places the owner of the vehicle financially responsible for the collision. The reporting party in the traffic accident is most likely the one who has both a *valid driver's license and insurance*. For this reason we need to ask them if they observed the driver of the other vehicle. Can they identify him/her if seen again? These questions appear basic, but many officers overlook them.

The license plate provided to you by the victim may appear at first to contain the proper information, but does it in fact belong to a vehicle of the same description? Comparison could quickly eliminate any follow-up if the numbers or letters in the vehicle's license plate number were partially transposed. Ask the witnesses and driver if they can tell you anything additional about the possible suspect vehicle, *e.g.* damage location or custom equipment. The suspect vehicle is most likely traveling through the streets of your city as you are still investigating the scene. The following will be a list of possible suspect vehicle information that might prove helpful to responding officers conducting the area check for the vehicle.

- *Year, make, and model of the vehicle*
- *Color and roof configuration, e.g. hard top, convertible, etc.*
- *Number of doors.*
- *Custom feature such as tinted windows, camper shells, wheels or tires, lowering or lifting equipment.*
- *Potential damage locations and paint transfer color from the victim's vehicle.*
- *Missing equipment left at the scene.*
- *Driver description if obtained*
- *Possible direction of travel for the suspect vehicle.*

CHECK THE SCENE CAREFULLY

Each agency has its own policy on how they will handle hit and run accidents. The Fontana Police Department, for example, will investigate only those hit and run accidents when substantial suspect information is present, *e.g. a license plate or driver lead.* This type of policy quickly *"cuts to the chase"* at a collision scene. A *property damage only report* is taken if the follow-up information is not gained. The remaining collisions have a possible suspect lead available. Again the most important aspect of this type of crime is *can the victim identify the suspected driver?* If this is the case, pieces of physical evidence remaining at the crime scene may be what you need to convince the suspected driver you are on the right track.

Carefully check and walk the entire crime scene. Many times the only real evidence of a traffic collision will be *paint transfers*. Depending on the severity of the impact, much larger substantial pieces of the suspect vehicle may have been torn off. This evidence is extremely important when you attempt to place the suspect vehicle at the collision scene. The registered owner or driver of the suspect vehicle will have a harder time trying to explain how this occurred. The vehicle debris may also fit the suspect vehicle similar to a *"jig saw puzzle."*

Start your search at the victim's vehicle. Check the damaged area first and look for any paint transfers that will point toward a definitive color of the suspect vehicle. This also will give the victim credibility if the paint matches his or her description of the color based on first hand observations. Verify your findings on the victim's vehicle and confirm the damage was new and a result of the current collision. Many people have been involved in previous collisions and have not repaired their vehicles.

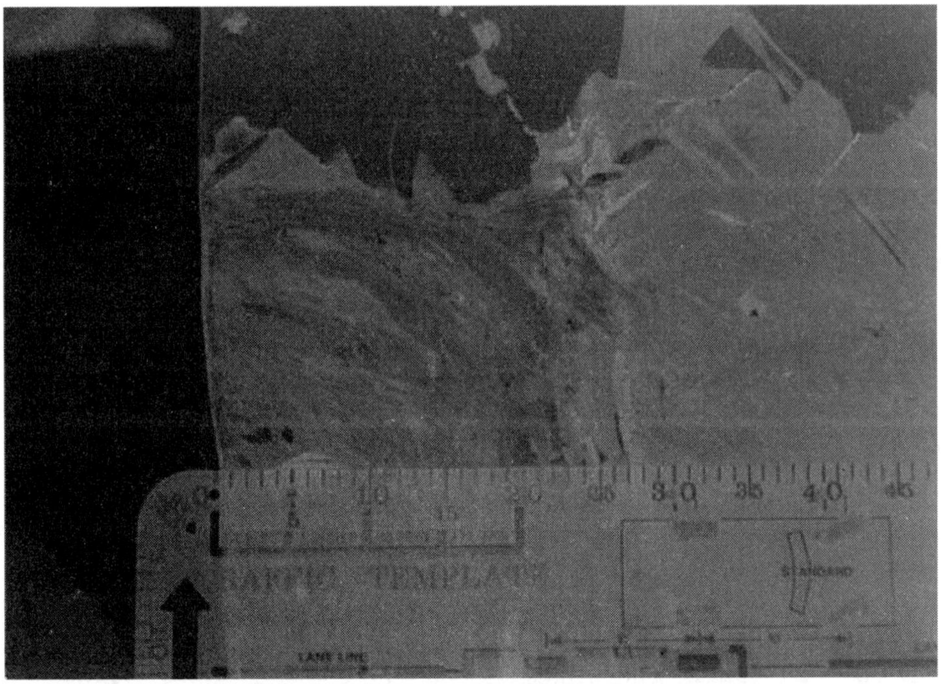

Photograph any paint transfers and collect a sample for comparison whenever possible.

Carefully inspect the damaged area for any signs of suspect vehicle debris imbedded in the vehicle. Impact can be very strong, and pieces of the suspect vehicle may actually still be attached to the victim's vehicle. Check the surrounding area and have the victim point toward the direction where the suspect fled. Pieces of the vehicle may have fallen onto the roadway as it left the scene. Locate and inspect the A.O.I. for any fluids, plastic, or glass debris. Fluid leakage is a good sign the suspect vehicle will not be traveling far after the collision. Many times radiator and transmission fluid have led the investigating officer, with nothing else to go on at the time, to the suspect vehicle.

Photograph and collect any physical evidence that will later become useful to your traffic detective. Mark and tag each item before it is placed into evidence. It is recommended that you make photocopies of the item, if practical, to allow the traffic detective the opportunity to visualize the missing pieces of the vehicle at the time of his or her follow-up. Use a ruler whenever possible in your photos which will give not only depth, but provide a realistic measurement for the District Attorney. Paint samples are especially important pieces of evidence depending on the priority of the case. Forensic specialists can compare paint samples from both the victim and suspect's vehicle. This inspection process also would be applied to a motorcycle, bicycle, and pedestrian traffic collision. Height of the damage, approach angle, and vehicle speeds are all-important when assessing the suspect vehicle in this type of collision.

EVIDENCE & THE FOLLOW-UP CONNECTION

The vehicle may be left at the scene allowing for a much more detailed vehicle inspection. The general rule is the suspect vehicle must be placed at the collision scene. Once this is accomplished, the vehicles must be placed together to prove a collision occurred. The driver of the suspect vehicle can then be put behind the wheel of the vehicle by a witness or other driver. This process becomes somewhat easier if the suspect vehicle remains at the scene due to being disabled or abandoned. The suspect vehicle can be thoroughly inspected by the officer completing two of these aforementioned steps. The damage will most likely match the victim's vehicle if the suspect vehicle was left at the scene.

Many clues as to the identity of the driver and how he/she can be placed behind the wheel of the suspect vehicle might be found in the vehicle itself. First check the registration to attempt a local follow-up. The registered owner's name and address may provide the officer with a potential driver's license match. This address may be more current than the vehicle information on the registration. Paperwork can often times be found in the vehicle that has a name and/or current address. The vehicle itself, *e.g.* seating position, steering wheel damage, and dashboard damage may be an indication the driver was possibly injured. The windshield may be cracked from the impact with the driver's head. This impact into the windshield may have left behind a small amount of human hair. Photograph and collect any relevant evidence.

As with any crime, the quicker the follow-up is performed, the better chance you have of catching the suspect. The inspection and evidence collection may be enough to convince a suspect he *has been placed at the scene*. His own injuries may match what you located in the suspect vehicle. Look for any injury that may have been sustained in a dashboard impact. Does the registered owner have a head injury consistent with the cracked windshield? A known case was solved by a strand of hair removed from the windshield of a suspect vehicle. This hair was matched to the suspect through microscopic inspection at the crime lab. The attention to detail is only as important as you choose to make it at the time of your initial collision report.

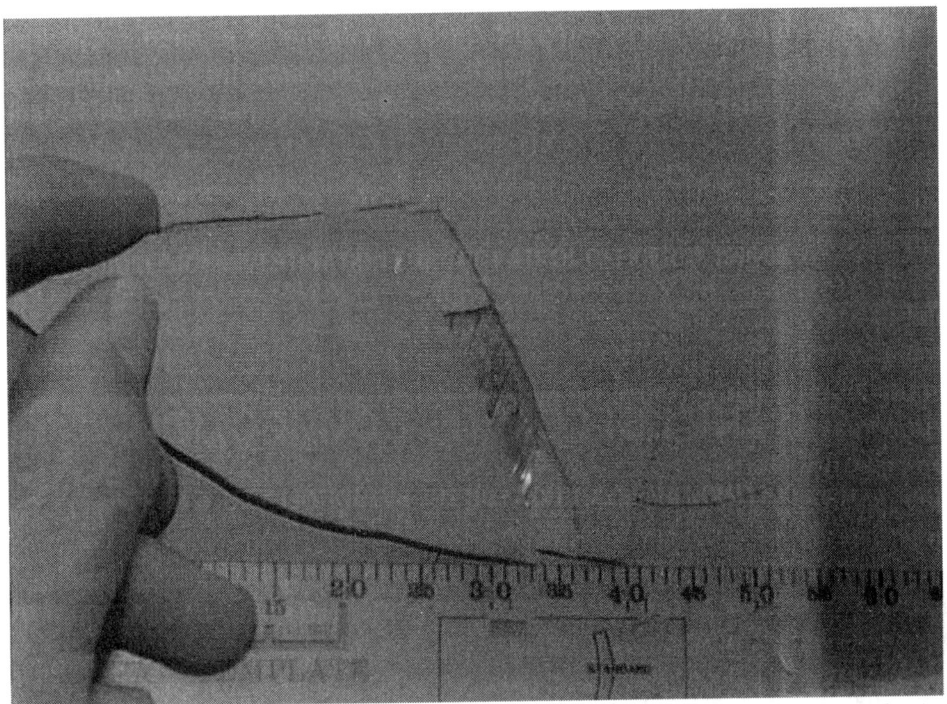

Carefully fit the pieces back together to compare the samples as in building a jigsaw puzzle.

Occasionally you will investigate a traffic collision with very few details about where or when the accident occurred. A citizen may contact your department about a possible collision that took place the night before when he/she was heavily intoxicated. Several pertinent facts of the collision are missing. Suspected drunk drivers have often waited until the following morning when he or she is certain the effects of the alcohol have worn off before reporting the *minor fender bender collision.* You will arrive and observe damage on the vehicle but have little or nothing else to go on. Before brushing off the damage as justified due to the driver's attitude, take a moment to reflect on the potential for solving another jurisdiction's hit and run. The damage alone may not be significant, but look closely for signs of a possible pedestrian accident. Small pieces of physical evidence such as skin or hair fragments may be found in the damaged area. This evidence may be the only link to the hit and run which will place this vehicle at the collision scene. Photograph, document, and consider sending teletypes to all surrounding police agencies notifying them of your information.

VEHICLE EVIDENCE STORAGE

The California Vehicle Code provides the authority for a peace officer to remove a vehicle for evidence. The purpose of this vehicle code section is to allow the investigating officer adequate time to properly inspect and collect any evidence necessary in a criminal case. Many officers utilize this section of the vehicle code to *hold the suspect vehicle as collateral* and leverage against the suspect. In other words, *"Come see me, and I will kick your car back to you."* Try to avoid using this section in the above-described fashion. Sometimes it may work, but other times an angry registered owner may sue the city and your agency will be forced to pay the tow bill and storage fees. It is recommended that you have the vehicles towed to the station where the inspection can be performed. Once this has been completed, make an attempt to contact the registered owner and note this on the tow form. Then have the vehicle towed back to the tow yard.

It is also recommended that you to contact your local district attorney's office and clarify how a fatal accident is to be handled concerning this issue. Many deputy district attorneys will rely on photographs of the vehicles. Others may insist the vehicles be made available to them for inspection and use in the trial. If this is the case, you may wish to store the vehicles at your police facility until the trial has been terminated.

SUSPECT CONTACT

You have completed the inspection at the scene of the accident and have responded to the registered owner's residence. Many times the owner is the suspected hit and run driver. Other times he or she may not be aware of the incident. Start with a very relaxed approach to the incident. Advise the owner of your investigation and how the information was obtained. The suspect vehicle may be in plain sight in the driveway or on the street. The damage may be a complete surprise the owner and therefore he may be a help in solving who was behind the wheel at the time of the collision. Ask the owner if he knows who drove the vehicle last. You have a fifty/fifty chance of gaining willing cooperation at this point. You must gauge the honesty of the registered owner at this point in your investigation. Advise the registered owner his vehicle can potentially be seized for the investigation of this crime. This may be just enough leverage against him to gain an admission of guilt in the incident. Miranda is not necessary, as he is not being detained and is free to leave whenever he chooses. Any statements or admissions made by the suspect are considered admissible as *"spontaneous statements."*

Again, suspects flee the accident scene for a variety of reasons. Explain the punishments in this type of case and assure the suspect he/she will not be arrested. This may be all you need to convince the suspected driver to be honest. If you promise a suspects you will not arrest them if they tell you the truth, you can still send the statement to the district attorney's office for a warrant at a later time. Do not make the assumption the owner of the vehicle was the suspected driver. The owner's relative, friend, co-worker, etc., may have damaged the vehicle outside of his or her presence.

If the registered owner of the vehicle is cooperative but denies any wrongdoing, simply gain as much information about him as possible. This might include where he was and who was in possession of his vehicle during the time period when the collision occurred. You will return to the station and attempt to put a photo line-up together for a witness or other involved driver. This will be the most reasonable way to clear the case when a witness to the incident exists.

If the suspect is willing to talk with you and admits he was present at the collision scene, don't stop with his statement alone. As in a D.U.I. investigation, we must prove the *corpus of the crime independent of his or her admission*. This may include inspecting the suspect vehicle utilizing a similar list as the one mentioned in Chapter 8. Photograph the suspect vehicle and any relevant damage. Ask the driver if this was the only damage his vehicle sustained in the accident. This will lock-in his statement about the vehicle and how the collision took place. Ask the suspect if anyone else was in the vehicle when the accident occurred. This will also help to eliminate any potential defense he or she may bring up at the time of trial. Once the case has been filed, many suspects suddenly become uncooperative and no longer wish to admit their guilt. A hit and run accident properly investigated will not provide a defense or loophole through which the suspect can escape.

FOLLOW-UP RESOURCES

Many of the hit and run traffic collisions you investigate will hinge on a photo line-up. The registered owner may match the general physical description of the suspect, but the witness could not be reached for a line-up. Many resources exist for you in collision follow-up. A photo line-up will be the quickest way of either identifying or eliminating a suspect. Photos can be gathered from a number of resources. San Bernardino, like many other counties in California, maintain *arrest-booking photos* at the Central Record's Station. The Department of Motor Vehicles maintains a file of many thousands of photos. This process can be made difficult only if the suspect's information is limited. A name from a registration combined with an address will yield reasonable results. The county's local booking system will most likely be your best resource. The San Bernardino County's booking system allows a search using only a name and general age. This may give you a start if this is the only information available to you at this time. This is in contrast to the state's DMV records management system that requires *exact* first name spelling. A county system will provide you with possible tattoos, recent addresses, and phone numbers.

Once you have located a possible suspect lead, check to see if a booking photo is available. If not, attempt to locate a DMV record with a photo file. Each agency in the state of California has a DMV code. This will allow you access to these records. Contact the Department of Motor Vehicles in Sacramento and request a photo of your potential suspect. DMV will also send you *"look alikes"* upon request. The photos at DMV are taken digitally and can be printed in color. These will be mailed to you in approximately two weeks.

Once the photos have been received, place a minimum of *six* photos in the line-up. Many officers routinely place the suspect in position number *three*. Avoid this whenever possible and vary the position of your suspect. This will again give you the appearance of being fair as possible. Admonish the victim in a similar manner as any other live line-up.

- This photo line-up contains 6 - 8 photos.
- The suspect who was the possible driver may or may not be observed in this line-up.
- The object of this line-up is to be fair to both the potential suspect and any parties involved. The decision is up to you.
- If you see the driver who caused this accident, *point* to him/her and identify the suspect by the number listed below their respective photo.

Once the photo line-up has been completed, attach a copy of the line-up to the report and book the original into evidence at your department.

FELONY VS. MISDEMEANOR

In California, a distinction lies between a felony and misdemeanor hit & run collision. This definition is left to the interpretation of the investigating officer. Section *20001(a) CVC* makes the action a *felony* if certain criteria are satisfied. The main difference between a *felony* and *misdemeanor* hit & run is the *injuries*. Drivers who claim *no injuries* will be the victims of a misdemeanor hit & run *20002(a) CVC*. Felony hit & run *20001(a) CVC* requires a *substantial injury*. This may include *severed limbs, severe internal injuries, or a combination of these*. The vehicle code does not dictate what type of injuries must be present to qualify the collision as a felony, but simply states the injuries must be substantial. A *complaint of pain* traffic collision does not appear to qualify per the above criteria. The accident investigator does not always know the status of the victim when the initial follow-up is being performed. This alone may give you the needed leverage when attempting to solve this type of crime. It is recommended that you do not book a suspect for *20001(a) CVC* based on a reported *complaint of pain* traffic collision. The reviewing district attorney is going to look for those *substantial* injuries mentioned earlier before he or she is willing to charge the suspect with the aforementioned felony section of *20001(a)CVC*.

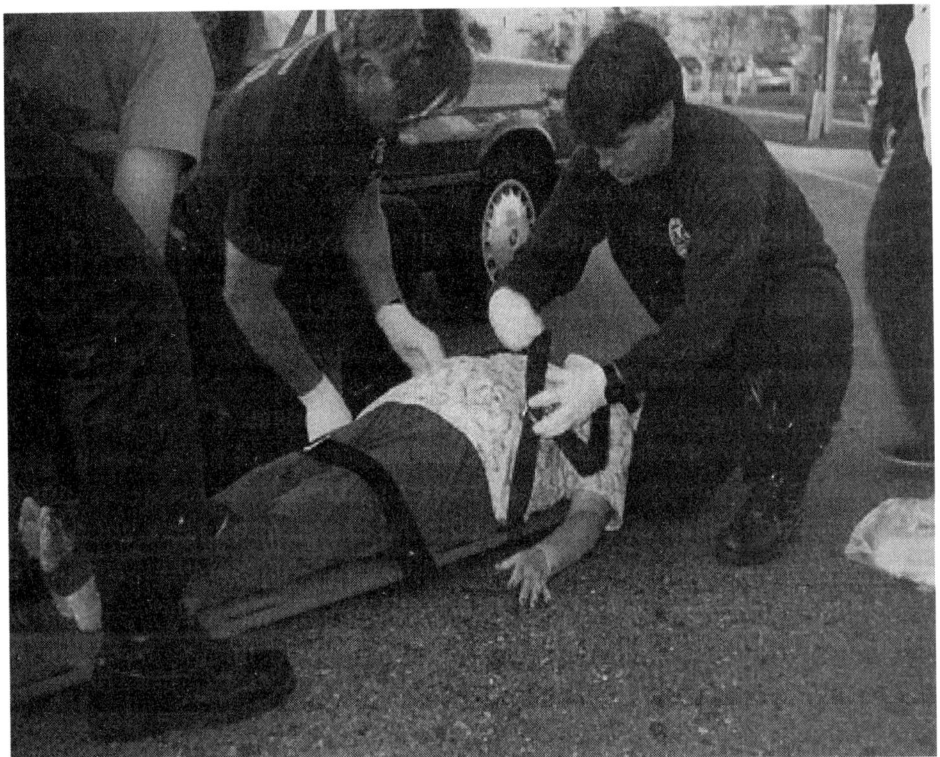

A felony Hit & Run conviction requires substantial injuries be inflicted on the victim in the collision.

If the victim of the collision has been injured severely, contact the hospital and attempt to get a preliminary evaluation of these injuries. The victim may not be conscious and therefore a summary of the injuries by the attending physician is acceptable. The district attorney will request the investigating officer re-contact the victim at a later time to confirm the status of these injuries. If the victim is conscious and willing to talk with you, ask them to sign and complete a *release of medical record form.* Many prosecutors are hesitant to file a felony charge of hit and run without all of this information.

Once the case has been sent to the district attorneys office, follow-up and contact the prosecutor reviewing the case. This follow-up may give him or her the needed push to file the case as you have requested. Ask the prosecuting attorney if you can assist them in any way with additional follow-up or if you can answer any of their questions. Many prosecutors will place the hit and run case on the *back burner* simply because they are uncomfortable with sifting through all of the pages of the medical record. If this is a problem, offer to complete a supplemental report of these records with a general synopsis.

INSURANCE FRAUD

Insurance fraud has been on the rise in the past few years. Many suspects and victims alike have little or no feeling for the insurance industry. For this reason, insurance fraud is tempting to the general law abiding citizen. Most see this as no different than cheating on your taxes. The law however, makes insurance fraud like any other fraud investigated by your agency. The majority of the public feels the insurance industry *has it coming to them*, and therefore they are not going to worry about a little loss on their behalf. What they don't realize is that the insurance industry is a billion dollar a year business which has a built in profit and loss margin. This means the industry passes their losses on to you the insurance consumer, who is required to have insurance.

Insurance fraud, as it is related to collision investigation, is restricted to the original call for service and your follow-up. This is the most critical time in this type of investigation. Many of the clues of this crime are readily apparent. However, the officer who is pressed to answer other calls may overlook them. Most of these collisions are processed by the insurance industry as a whole, and due to the sheer volume of claims, also are overlooked. This does not change the claim to payment ratio for rate adjustment. For this reason, if no other, you are also charged with this extra responsibility.

Many of the clues of insurance fraud are evident in how the suspect claims the incident took place. Review his/her story of how the incident occurred. Compare the damage to what they claim could have happened. Ask yourself some of the questions below and ask the reporting party to justify their answers. Each of these should raise a *red flag* in your mind if the answers are not what you would expect.

- Were there any witnesses to this *single vehicle collision*?
- Why did the driver *wait to report* this accident until now?
- Does the *damage appear to match* what the suspect/driver is telling you?
- Is the driver of the vehicle *insured*?
- Can he/she *accurately* describe where the collision took place? This would include all relevant landmarks, etc.
- Does he/she have any information about the vehicle that fled the scene? The majority will not have this information, therefore limiting your ability to follow-up any leads.
- Was the driver or any injured passenger seen at a local hospital? The majority of suspects will choose a hospital out of the area, taking a chance you will not call them.

Many other questions can also be asked to verify the story you are being provided. The majority of reporting parties in these falsely reported accidents are counting on your disinterested approach to accident investigation. They will not appear to really care how the accident took place and will try to convince you they were *true victims* in this whole situation.

The questions above are a guide which will help you differentiate between the real victim and the suspect who would like to do nothing more than report the incident and get out of there. Some suspects will even act *upset* with you for asking these questions and at times pressing for more information. The real victims will understand if you explain the reason for this additional information.

You may investigate a hit and run accident where you locate the suspect who did not have an apparent reason for leaving the scene as outlined in the earlier part of this chapter. In some cases they may tell you that he/she simply did not want to have the accident reported to his/her insurance company. This should also send up a *red flag* in your mind. Ask the suspect for his/her insurance information. Follow-up by contacting the person's insurance company. Many times the suspect has already called the insurance company and reported he/she was the victim of a hit and run accident, not counting on the fact you would locate them.

The California Insurance Code requires insurance companies to cooperate with any law enforcement agency that is investigating potential insurance fraud. This would include turning over any and all *original* files they maintain. In a case, as mentioned above, the suspect did report he was the victim of a hit and run which occurred in another Jurisdiction. The driver stated he did not call the police department because he had no suspect information. The suspect's insurance company had a transcript of the call and all relevant information ready for the investigating officer to pick-up in the days following the investigation.

The suspect was later charged with *felony insurance fraud* and sentenced to several months in jail. The key to successful insurance fraud investigations is reading the reports carefully and asking simple logical questions. Again, the suspects in this type of crime are looking for the officers to take a quick report and send it to file. They are not counting on the sharp, well-versed officer to start asking questions which will delay the process by the insurance company. San Bernardino County for example has a division at the Central District Attorney's Office that specializes in insurance fraud. They are a great resource if a question arises which needs some direction. The insurance companies also have investigators which work for them, however they themselves will tell you their hands are somewhat tied. The insurance company itself sees this as a *no-win situation* for prosecution. They do not recover any funds in this process and therefore are reluctant to put much emphasis in this area of the business. This however, should not preclude you from delving into this area of police work for the experience.

THIS PAGE INTENTIONALLY LEFT BLANK

12

COURTROOM PREPARATION & TESTIMONY

PRESENTING YOUR CASE

Arrests are made and reports are completed everyday detailing the events surrounding incidents we are involved in. These reports outline the *corpus* of the crime and any relevant *witness statements* or *evidence* collected at the crime scene. The report you complete in any given event is all the Deputy District Attorney will have to guide him or her through the facts of the case. The organizational skills utilized in your case will represent your sheriff or police department as a whole. Many officers complete reports and are quickly detached from the case. The report you complete at the scene is reviewed several times by *Sergeants, Traffic Detectives, and even the staff of your respective departments.* A majority of the reports you complete move smoothly through the system without any restrictions; however others will be reviewed by the City Attorney. For this reason a professional product is essential.

In traffic investigation, a unique set of circumstances exists. The collision report is forwarded to the district attorney's office like any other report; however, many Deputy District Attorneys are very uncomfortable with collision investigations in general. Most Deputy DA's have limited experience in handling major traffic related manslaughter cases. They will rely on the expertise you represent in your investigative report. To them, you are the expert in collision investigation. For this reason, they will call upon you to guide them through preparing for the preliminary hearing and even the jury trial. One advantage to this is the defense attorney's office will also be uncomfortable with this type of case.

Your report and investigation must be both accurate and *fair*. The collision investigator must present the view he or she is being *very impartial* in the determination of what caused the collision. Even the most experienced collision investigator must write his or her report in a way that the *layman* will understand it. This would include simple explanations of the vehicle code and how you determined which party violated the specific section at hand. Courtroom preparation also includes preparing for your case in even the simplest collisions. A traffic collision with an infraction violation will be the responsibility of the investigating officer to present in traffic court at the time of the court trial. An infraction violation citation in most counties will not be the type of case in which the

District Attorney's office will become involved. You will be responsible for contacting the victims and witnesses, etc.

PROFESSIONAL APPEARANCE

Courtroom preparation and testimony begins before you leave your residence or locker room. Each agency has a policy as to the attire worn to courtroom appearances. This may include wearing the departmentally approved uniform or professional business attire, such as a *business suit or equivalent for female officers*. Each officer will make a determination in which type of attire he or she feels most comfortable at the time. The pride you take in your appearance will have a direct reflection of how you are perceived not only by the jury, but also by the attending attorneys. An officer who dresses well in either a business suit or departmental uniform will give the representation he or she is very well prepared and articulate.

The television industry would like everyone to believe we have little or no pride when appearing in uniform or court. The majority of television shows viewed weekly by the public reflect the officers looking less than professional and completely out of the time period. We know that television is far from accurate in representing law enforcement at large. The public however, gains its perspective of law enforcement from television more than any other resource. If for no other reason, as professionals we must make a very favorable impression on the public and our fellow colleagues as well.

Dress professionally and look sharp when you appear in court. When an officer takes the stand in a suit or uniform that looks like he/she slept in it the night before, it reflects on all law enforcement officers. Your appearance will impact all other officers when we take the stand and testify at a later time.

CASE REVIEW

Arrive early for your courtroom appearance and review your case. Many officers wait until the day they appear in court to review their reports. Some officers arrive for work or court, quickly grab a police unit, and look at the report on their way to court. This will not provide you with the much-needed time to absorb the details of the case. It is recommended that you pull the case at least the day before and review it several times. This will give you a more relaxed feeling on the day of your court appearance. Your lack of preparation in reviewing the report will be evident while you are on the stand. You will continually need to refer to the report to refresh your memory. If at all possible, even review the scene of the collision and check the intersection for any changes. Remember, the prosecution must present their case beyond a reasonable doubt.

The defense may have several exhibits that will serve to only weaken the prosecutor's case. A thorough investigation on your part may close those gaps or holes in the case.

Contact the deputy DA prior to the day you are to appear and ask if any other follow-up of the case needs to be done. They will often not review the case until the day of trial and will be looking to you for the strong and weak points of the case. Be frank and honest with the deputy DA when discussing the case. Point out the possible trouble spots in the case. He or she will then be prepared for the confrontation over this issue when it arises.

Be prepared for court by reviewing your report before court.

COURTROOM DEMEANOR

The way you carry yourself in a courtroom setting is equally as important as your appearance. Being fair and impartial is very important. You must find a happy medium between *"confidence"* and *"cockiness."* Many officers have very little experience in this area. Depending on the court process in your area, many of you will only actually follow the process to a jury trial on a limited basis. Most of the cases are adjudicated at the preliminary trial level in a *plea bargain arrangement.*

Approaching the stand:

- Approach the stand confidently with your shoulders square and your head held up high. Stand facing the court clerk and make eye contact with him or her while responding to the oath. The jury panel is watching very closely and will make their first decisions about your professionalism at this stage in the process.

The witness stand:

- Sit comfortably on the stand but don't slouch. Adjust the microphone to your mouth and place the copy of your report in a position to access it easily. Place your hands in your lap, which will keep you from talking with them if you become nervous.

Listen to the question:

- Take the time to carefully listen to the question before answering. Some questions only require a *yes* or *no* response from you. Others will be framed in such a way a simple yes or no will not fully explain your position. Ask the defense attorney or prosecutor to *"please repeat the question."* This will give you the opportunity to re-think your response.

Speaking and answering questions:

- Speak naturally and don't mumble when giving your answers. Listen to the questions carefully and take a moment to frame your answer. The general rule is not to elaborate beyond the scope of the question. This only provides the defense attorney with additional areas in which to cross examine-you.

- Stay away from *"police jargon"* when addressing the jury. The jury will not be impressed with this type of explanation of what occurred. Much of this type of jargon can lose the jury's interest in your answer.

- Be fair as possible to *both* attorneys. This will give you the appearance of not taking this specific case *"personally."* Many jurors truly believe the charges you have made are *"drummed up."*

Conversations off the stand:

- You never know who might be eavesdropping on your conversation outside of the courtroom. Witnesses for the defense or even a defense attorney's investigator may be within earshot of you. An off-color joke about the defendant or attorney may come back full circle to haunt you on the stand after the break.

- *Nothing* is *"off the record"* when on-duty and discussing the case in an open forum. Many defense attorneys will approach you during the break and attempt to casually discuss the case. Jurors may view this as inappropriate during the trial.

GAMES PEOPLE PLAY

Many officers see the court system as a game between the lawyers and the officers, with a judge as the referee. The jurors often give the impression they are completely lost and did not appear to have heard any of the testimony. Each of the parties in a courtroom has a specific job in the process. You, as the investigator, are a witness for the state. The District Attorney is present to prosecute or present the *people's case against the defendant.* The prosecutor's job is to make the evidence as easy to understand as possible. He or she must *"put on the case"* in a logical, easy-to-follow order according to the rules of admissibility.

By contrast, the defense attorney's job is to create doubt in any or all of the people's case. He or she will do just about anything to disrupt the logical easy to understand order of the case. Most defense attorney's will not argue the innocence or guilt of their client, but instead attempt to exclude evidence including any gained statements, therefore removing one of the major building blocks in the case. For this reason you, as the officer (witness for the people), must be prepared for this *"game of wit."* Preparation for the courtroom is essential to this process. This is not a criticism of the role defense attorneys play in the courtroom, but a guide to the most common approaches used by the defense.

Leading questions:

- Attorneys will often attempt to make their point with the jury by asking a question they already know the answer to. They are simply asking a witness to affirm this point by the way the question is framed. Witnesses will be asked a question that may have more than one answer and be asked for a simple *"yes"* or *"no."* This cannot always be accomplished. Advise the attorney the question cannot be answered in this fashion and wait to see if he/she asks a clearer follow-up question.

Hostile offensive questions:

- Remain calm on the stand if this type of question is asked of you. The attorney is looking to provoke you into a planned response. Attorneys learn to challenge a solid witness and attempt to *"rattle"* him/her, making it more difficult to maintain their composure in the process. This type of approach can backfire on the attorney if the witness is not rattled. This can be used in your favor if the attorney himself becomes upset because you remain calm and don't show any response toward him/her.

Surprise Questions:

- Defense attorneys also have investigators on their side. These investigators will uncover evidence that sometimes may hurt your case. Therefore, act calm and non-emotional on the stand if a question arises which you know is detrimental to the case as a whole. The attorney may choose not to pursue this avenue if he feels you are prepared for the questions at hand.

Refreshing your memory:

- You are not expected to have all of the answers to every question. The jury expects you to be human. You may look like you have all of the answers and are too well prepared if you never need to look at the report during cross-examination. Consider asking to refresh your memory at least once during the course of the trial. This will provide you the opportunity to slow down and pace yourself during a long cross-examination.

Evidence:

- Both the prosecutor and defense attorney may ask you to identify evidence obtained at the scene. This will allow the evidence to be admitted into the trial. Many officers fail to review all relevant evidence before trial and are not fully prepared for these questions at trial. A detective is not always assigned to this type of case and therefore you will be responsible for this part of the trail. Be careful in identifying items that require personal knowledge. Give approximations and not exact measurements when asked for distance estimates in collision related criminal proceedings.

- Testify the *"evidence pointed toward"* and not *"I think"* when asked for your potential expert opinion. Also state the item *"appeared"* rather than *"it was."* These types of answers will again give you the appearance of being very impartial.

Unknowns:

- Many officers feel they must answer the question because the answer itself was not included in the initial report. This is a time to truly prove yourself on the stand and come across as *honest*. Don't be afraid to say, *"I don't know."* Jurors respect an officer who can admit; *"he doesn't know everything."*

TRAFFIC COURT TRIALS

Earlier it was mentioned that you may be solely responsible for putting on a court trial involving a citation written as the result of a collision investigation. The investigating officer must understand he or she *was not a witness to the events surrounding the collision* and therefore cannot testify to the incident itself. The California Vehicle Code allows you as the investigating officer to issue a *"written notice to appear"* after completing a basic collision investigation class. Occasionally the party found most at fault decides to plead *"not guilty"* and asks for a court trial. You will receive a subpoena for the court trial in the same fashion as any other written citation, however this type of trial requires a great deal more preparation.

You must contact the witnesses in the case and ask to appear in court to provide their account of the collision. Your subpoena may arrive several months after the collision first occurred. Contacting a witness is not the most challenging aspect of the process. In fact many witnesses are more than happy to hear from you. They; however have returned to their daily lives and wish to put the incident behind them. For this reason, they no longer are interested in assisting you in the case by confronting the party at fault *one more time*. Without a witness in the case, the judge has no other choice but to dismiss the case against the defendant.

Contact your local District Attorney's office and ask for their assistance in this matter. If they decline due to the caseload, you must be prepared to handle this task on your own. If you are able to gain the willing participation from the witness, ask him/her if he/she can testify on your behalf. Ask the witness to meet you one-half hour before the court trial is to begin. Assemble a short list of simple questions for him/her to answer at the court trial. You will be asking the questions in an informal atmosphere during the court trial. Many judges understand the challenge you are facing and will often times ask questions themselves to facilitate this process.

THE VERDICT

The judge or hearing officer has a difficult job to perform in a contested court trial over a citation. Police officers feel the defendant should always be found guilty based on the testimony at hand. The judge however must rule on *"does reasonable doubt exist?"* Here are some interesting points offered by a traffic commissioner. First, the officer is a witness and not a prosecutor in the courtroom. For that reason alone, the officer (witness) may not be allowed to ask questions of another witness. The officer is placed in a very precarious position in his courtroom. The officer must balance the role of being a prosecutor with the role of being a witness.

The judge places him or herself in the middle between all parties involved. Their role is to insure the rules of law are strictly followed.

The judge or commissioner must make the decision based on the evidence presented before him. The defendant is allowed to ask follow-up questions of the officer and has the ability to *represent himself.* He cannot be forced to *testify against himself.* The verdict does not always go in the favor of the officer. Occasionally the defendant *does* create just enough doubt to favor a *"not guilty verdict."* This is not meant to diminish the officer's testimony, officers should not take it personally. Remember, traffic investigation and enforcement should be handled as *"impartial as possible."* Some officers feel their job is completed when the defendant *signs the citation in the field.* For this reason, the court trial is a process where questions can be asked of you and about the facts surrounding your initial observations. Answer the questions in a respectful manner without sounding sarcastic toward the defendant. The judge may understand your concerns but may also weigh the defendant's understanding of the law at hand.

Take your time and include all of the relevant facts. Don't *assume* the judge is familiar with the area of the traffic stop. Adding facts about the other vehicles affected by the violation always adds credibility to your case. If the judge does ask questions of you, he is attempting to clarify an issue in the case. Once the verdict is rendered, act professional even if the case is dismissed. The judge and entire courtroom is watching for your reaction to this verdict. Think about your courtroom trials over the past few years. The odds are in your favor if the evidence is presented properly.

THIS PAGE INTENTIONALLY LEFT BLANK

FORMULA WORK SHEET

The following formulas can be found in Chapter 10 Basic Skidmark Analysis. Each of these formulas may be used or manipulated algebraically to assist the investigator in solving for the needed missing element.

	What I want to know:	***What I have:***	***Formula***
1.	**Drag factor** (*f*)	*S* = *Speed* *d* = Distance *f* = Friction	$f = \frac{S^2}{30df}$
2.	**Drag factor** (*f*)	F = Force	$f = \frac{F}{w}$
3.	**Slide to stop**	*S* = Speed *(mph)* d = Distance f = friction	$S = \sqrt{30df}$
4.	**Slide to Stop**	*V* = Velocity (fps) *a* = Acceleration *d* = Distance	$V = \sqrt{2ad}$
5.	**Acceleration**	*g = Gravity 32.2 fps²* *f = friction*	$a = gf$
6.	**Radius**	C = Chord *r* = radius m = Middle ordinate	$R = \frac{C^2}{8m} + \frac{m}{2}$
7.	**Critical Speed**	S = Speed (mph) r = radius *f* = friction e = elevation %	$S = 3.86\sqrt{r(f \pm e)}$
8.	**Distance**	*S = Speed* *d = Distance*	$d = \frac{S^2}{30f}$
9.	**Distance**	*V = Velocity* *t = Time*	$d = Vt$
10.	**Velocity in (fps)**	*S = Speed (mph)*	$V = S(1.467)$
11.	**Speed (mph)**	*V = Velocity*	$S = V(.6818)$

Symbol Interpretation

These formulas refer to several symbols. They can be interpreted as follows.

- *S = Speed in miles per hour or* (mph)
- *V = Velocity in* (fps)
- *d = Distance measured in feet and inches*
- *f = Friction or drag factor coefficient*
- *r= Radius in feet*
- *e = % of grade* ±
  e.g. *3% ascending = .03 added to the drag factor coefficient;* 3% descending = *.03 subtracted from the drag factor*
- *t = Time in seconds*
- *a = Acceleration*

DRAG FACTOR / COEFFICIENT OF FRICTION CHART

The friction and drag factor can be calculated using a *drag sled*, or you may wish to use the friction values in this table.

Description of Roadway Surface	*Dry* Less than 30 mph	*Dry* More than 30 mph	*Wet* Less than 30 mph	*Wet* More than 30 mph
1. Concrete				
New & Sharp	.80 - 1.00	.70 - .85	.50 - .80	.40 - .75
Traveled	.60 - .80	.60 - .80	.45 - .70	.45 - .65
Traffic polished	.55 - .75	.50 - .65	.45 - .65	.45 - .60
2. Asphalt or Tar				
New & Sharp	.80 - 1.00	.65 - .70	.50 - .80	.45 - .75
Traveled	.60 - .80	.40 - .70	.45 -.70	.40 - .65
3. Gravel				
Packed, oiled	.55 - .85	.50 - .80	.40 - .80	.40 - .60
Loose	.40 - .70	.40 - .70	.45 - .75	.45 - .75
4. Ice				
Smooth	.10 - .25	.07 - .20	.05 - .10	.05 - .10
5. Snow				
Packed	.30 - .55	.35 - .55	.30 - .60	.30 - .60

References

- General yearly reports, ***The Office of Traffic Safety***, Sacramento California.
- S.W.I.T.R.S., Feb. 1998 Complete Revision ***The California Highway Patrol***, Sacramento California.
- The Public Safety Forum, ***America On-Line***, New York 1996.
- Hazardous Materials Handling, ***P.O.S.T. Module 1 & 2***, Sacramento California.
- Photography, an Investigative Tool, ***International Chiefs of Police 1968***, NW Washington DC.
- Photography, ***Webster's New World Dictionary***, New York
- The California Vehicle Code, ***The department of Motor Vehicles 1996***, Sacramento California.
- DUI, ***The San Bernardino County Sun Newspaper 1996***, San Bernardino California.
- The California Peace Officers Legal Resource Book, ***The California Department of Justice***, Sacramento California.
- Basic Collision Analysis & Scene Documentation, ***David Casteel & Steven Moss***, San Diego California.
- The Traffic Accident Investigation Manual, ***J. Stannard & Lynn Fricke***, Northwestern Traffic Institute.
- P.O.S.T. Basic Accident Investigation Handouts, ***P.O.S.T.***, Sacramento California.
- P.O.S.T. Reconstruction Handouts, ***P.O.S.T.***, Sacramento California.

NOTES